TOTAL COMMUNICATION

TOTAL COMMUNICATION

**The Meaning Behind the Movement
to Expand Educational Opportunities
for Deaf Children**

By

JAMES ALON PAHZ, M.S., M.P.H.

*Assistant Professor of Health Education
Central Michigan University
Mount Pleasant, Michigan*

and

CHERYL SUZANNE PAHZ

With a Chapter by

Glenn T. Lloyd, Ed.D.

*Professor of Special Education
Lenoir Rhyne College
Hickory, North Carolina
President
American Deafness and Rehabilitation Association
Editor
Journal of Rehabilitation of the Deaf*

CHARLES C THOMAS • PUBLISHER
Springfield • Illinois • U.S.A.

Published and Distributed Throughout the World by

CHARLES C THOMAS ● PUBLISHER

Bannerstone House

301-327 East Lawrence Avenue, Springfield, Illinois, U.S.A.

© *1978, by* CHARLES C THOMAS ● PUBLISHER

ISBN 0-398-03784-1

Library of Congress Catalog Card Number: 77-28135

With THOMAS BOOKS *careful attention is given to all details of
manufacturing and design. It is the Publisher's desire to present books that
are satisfactory as to their physical qualities and artistic possibilities and
appropriate for their particular use.* THOMAS BOOKS *will be true to those
laws of quality that assure a good name and good will.*

Printed in the United States of America
R-1

Library of Congress Cataloging in Publication Data

Pahz, Jim.
  Total communication.

  Bibliography: p.
  Includes index.
  1. Deaf--Education. 2. Deaf--Means of communica-
tion. I. Pahz, Cheryl Suzanne, joint author.
II. Lloyd, Glenn T., joint author. III. Title.
HV2430.P33   371.9'12   77-28135,
ISBN 0-398-03784-1

to
Katherine and Abraham Goldfeder
and
Shirley and Morris McConnell

Parents with Energy and Vision

INTRODUCTION

WHY choose *Total Communication* as a topic of study?

Some time ago, before we began writing this book, we noticed a great deal of interest in the subject of *Total Communication*. We saw definitions printed on a regular basis in several publications, and we heard the term being used or misused among our acquaintances; such persons included teachers, administrators, and deaf persons.

Two things are readily apparent from the discussions: First, no two people seemed to agree fully on what Total Communication really was (despite the printed definitions); second, intense emotions were elicited from people discussing the subject.

With regard to our first observation, we too were ignorant of what Total Communication really entailed. We did not, for instance, know whether or not it was distinguishable from the "combined system" or, for that matter, the "simultaneous approach." Actually, we could not even distinguish the latter two from each other!

One reason, then, for writing this book was to find out precisely what Total Communication really was all about — where it came from; what it purported to do; and what it would not be able to accomplish.

Returning to our second observation, the degree of emotions generated when people discussed Total Communication, we can only say that since we started this project such emotionalism has continued to manifest itself. In showing our preliminary draft to several persons, the comment was frequently made that perhaps the cartoons from the *Deaf Spectrum* should be eliminated. The reason was given that "they were too emotional" and, therefore, detracted from "objectivity." Interestingly enough, Mr. Hemstreet, cartoonist for the *Deaf Spectrum*, as well as most of the staff, is deaf. We felt this to be significant. As we indicated, Total Communication is an emotional issue. We decided a book on Total Communication had to have a place for such cartoons if the reader was to understand some of the frustrations deaf persons have experienced as seen through their own eyes. Furthermore, such cartoons help elucidate the reasons why so many persons have embraced the philosophy of Total Communication with such a degree of enthusiasm.

That Total Communication is a very emotional issue should not be surprising. The issue grows directly out of the methodological controversy that has been the hallmark of the education of deaf children. Those who advocate Total Communication are not more emotional in their pronouncements than those who previously advocated the combined system or the oral system. You cannot remain aloof when you are dealing with the lives of deaf children, and it is hard to hide one's enthusiasm when a philosophy such as Total Communication, which so greatly enhances the deaf child's opportunities to learn, is known.

J.A.P.
C.S.P.

ACKNOWLEDGMENTS

W E would like to express our gratitude to all those persons who helped us to write this book. We are very grateful to Mr. Clarence Supalla of the *Deaf Spectrum* for allowing us to reproduce material from his publication, and also to Mr. Dudley Hemstreet, cartoonist for the *Deaf Spectrum* staff, who permitted us to use his creative materials. Ms. Corrine Hilton of the Edward Miner Gallaudet Memorial Library was extremely helpful to us in securing the photographic reproductions we sought. Mr. Albert G. Barnabei, Convention Chairman of the New Jersey Association of the Deaf, was also helpful in sending materials pertaining to Total Communication activities in his state.

We are especially grateful to Dr. Glenn Lloyd, who helped us with his continual support throughout this project. We feel very honored to have his contribution included with our efforts.

We have received helpful suggestions from other persons who read our manuscript in its preparatory stage. Among those to whom we would like to express our gratitude are: Ms. Loraine J. DiPietro and Mr. Albert T. Pimentel from Gallaudet College; Dr. William J. McClure, Director of the Florida School for the Deaf and Blind; and Mr. Frederick C. Schreiber, Executive Secretary of the National Association of the Deaf.

J.A.P.
C.S.P.

CONTENTS

TOTAL COMMUNICATION

CHAPTER 1

EDUCATING DEAF CHILDREN
A Brief Historical Perspective

ANCIENT AND MEDIEVAL TIMES

ALTHOUGH there are few facts regarding treatment of deaf persons in antiquity, it is certain that life was not easy for individuals with any type of handicapping condition during this period of history. Historical records show that, among primitive people, those who were unable to contribute to the needs of the tribe were not allowed to live. Deformed or weak infants were often destroyed at birth.[1] Plutarch, in his description of Spartan training, wrote that such a child was "thrown into the place called Apothetae, which is a deep cavern near the mountain Taygetus, concluding that its life could be no advantage either to itself or to the public, since nature had not given it at first any strength or goodness of constitution."[2]

Since most deaf infants today appear normal and progress through babbling stages similar to hearing children, it is doubtful that their handicap would be discovered during the first two years of life. However, according to Dionysius of Halicarnassus, the early Roman practice was to murder any child at the age of three who appeared likely to become a liability of the state.[3] At this age, a child's deafness could have been apparent.

At any rate, it is safe to assume that the birth of a handicapped child in early communities was a burden and, perhaps, even a family disgrace in the eyes of tribal society.[4]

The early Hebrews were among the first to look upon the deaf person with compassion. The earliest known attempt to legislate for protection of deaf people is found in Hebrew Law: "Thou shalt not curse the deaf, nor put a stumbling block before the blind, but shalt fear thy God."[5]

In general, the Hebrew attitude toward deaf persons seems to have been one of tolerance. It was considered society's duty to protect and shelter unfortunates.[6]

An interesting facet of the Hebrew Law concerning the non-hearing minority was the distinction made between those who could hear but could not speak, and those who could speak but not hear. Both these classes had rights and obligations. Only those deaf and dumb were regarded as children by the Law.[7]

Eventually, the distinctions were passed over into Roman law, and under the Emperor Justinian (530 AD), five classes of infirmity were recognized:

1. The deaf and dumb with both infirmities congenital
2. The deaf and dumb from causes arising since birth
3. The congenitally deaf but not dumb
4. The deaf only, from causes arising since birth
5. The dumb only, whether from congenital or causes arising since birth.[8]

With respect to legal responsibility, only those congenitally deaf and dumb were without rights and responsibilities.[9]

Unfortunately, this early concern for the legal status of the deaf population did little to aid the actual understanding of deafness or its implications. It was centuries before the relationship between hearing and speech was understood. For example, the great physician Hippocrates of Cos (460 BC) stated that the lack of speech in those persons deaf from birth was evidence that intelligible speech depended upon proper action of the tongue.[10] Centuries later, Claudius Galen (170 AD) proposed that speech and hearing shared a common source in the brain and that an injury to this source resulted in both deafness and dumbness.[11]

Part of the lack of understanding may have been due to the scarcity of anatomical knowledge concerning the ear. There was at this time a reluctance to perform human dissections, and the ear itself was difficult to study because of its small size and inaccessibility. Consequently, ancient and medieval study of the ear was concerned with outer ear trouble and whatever middle ear disease that could be reached from the external auditory meatus.[12] As a result, undue importance was placed upon the outer ear and led to such inaccurate conclusions as the one posed by Aristotle: "Some [ears] are fine, some are coarse, and some are of medium texture: the last kind are the best for hearing."[13]

Although this assumption may be regarded with amusement in the light of modern knowledge, other earlier misconceptions cannot be so lightly dismissed. For example, another conclusion — also by Aristotle — had disastrous results for deaf people.

> Men that are deaf are in all cases also dumb; that is, they can make vocal sounds, but they cannot speak. Children, just as they have no control over other parts, so have no control, at first, over the tongue; but it is so far imperfect, and only frees and detaches itself by degrees, so that in the interval children for the most part lisp and stutter.[14]

Due to distorted translations, this statement came to read: "Those who are born deaf all become senseless and incapable of reason."[15] Since Aristotle's writings were generally accepted as authoritative throughout the Middle Ages, those who were deaf were considered unreachable, for no educated man would waste his time on an "acknowledged impossibility."[16]

At this point, it should be noted there is evidence that deaf people had developed a language of gestures and signs in ancient times.[17] Socrates (386 BC), in a discussion with Hermogenes and Cratylus, commented, "If we had neither voice nor tongue, and yet wished to manifest things to one another, should we not, like those which are at present mute, endeavor to signify our meaning by the hands, head, and other parts of the body?"[18]

At a much later date, Augustine in *De Quantitate Anima* mentions a young deaf-and-dumb man who understood others only by their gestures.[19] So, although sign language existed among deaf people and no doubt among some hearing people, its potential for education was not explored.[20]

It should be remembered that education, even for the general population, was limited at that time, and the scarcity of books necessitated any teaching for the most part to be done orally.[21] As Kenneth Hodgson points out, "A world which saw nothing wrong in abandoning most of its population to untutored ignorance naturally did not remark the neglect of the deaf. The idea of abandoning the deaf was not only tolerated: any other notion would have seemed absurd."[22]

This attitude toward education, coupled with Aristotle's unfortunate pronouncement concerning the "senselessness" of those deaf, was to hold back progress for the deaf population for several centuries.

SIXTEENTH CENTURY

In the sixteenth century several events contributing to an educational breakthrough for deaf people occurred. One of these was the revolutionary declaration made by Girolamo Cardano (1501-1576) of Milan. In the book entitled *Paralipomenon,* he stated, "We can accomplish that a deaf mute hear by reading and speak by writing."[23]

This pronouncement directly contradicted the writing of Aristotle which had for so long been an obstacle to the education of those who were deaf. Because of Cardano, deaf people were now considered educable.[24]

Proof of Cardano's theory was provided by one of the first recorded teachers of deaf children, Pedro Ponce de Leon.[25] A spanish monk, Ponce de Leon became interested in teaching deaf persons out of his concern for their salvation. The church's attitude toward deaf persons was chiefly derived from the text of Romans 10:17: "So faith cometh from what is heard."[26] It was Ponce's hope to remove this obstacle to salvation by teaching deaf persons to perform oral prayers and confession. Consequently, his teaching was aimed toward the production of speech.[27]

Pedro Ponce de Leon was supported in his speech-teaching efforts by his students' parents, but for much more practical reasons. Since his students were from the noble families of Spain, many were heirs to great estates; yet as deaf-mutes, they were to remain legally as infants. Naturally, this was disastrous to the families, since it could alter the descent of a title and fortune. However, as noted earlier, Roman law recognized those who were deaf but able to speak as persons capable of discharging legal obligations.[28]

The wealth of the great families of Spain was tremendous during the 1500s, and with such fortunes at stake, it is easy to see why they were eager to attempt the "impossible."[29] Pedro Ponce de Leon appears to have been quite successful at achieving the goal of speech. It is written that he taught his students to speak with "extraordinary perfection."[30]

Other teachers of deaf children arose at this time to instruct the offspring of the wealthy. The success of these early teachers is no doubt due in part to the small number of students whom they taught and the fact they were well paid to devote their whole attention to the education of a child over a period of years.[31]

An item of interest concerning the education of deaf persons that appeared in the sixteenth century is the following "miracle cure" reported by a physician from Avignon named Pietro di Castro.

> First the deaf-mute was to purge himself with hellebore. Then the hair on the crown of his head was shaven, and a salve was applied. This salve was composed of saltpetre, nitre, almond oil, brandy, and naphtha, and was to be applied at night. In the morning it was washed off and his hair was combed. When one spoke strongly then, to the crown of his head, he could perceive voice, and so learn to speak.[32]

SEVENTEENTH CENTURY

In the seventeenth century there was a growing recognition of education as a means of improving man's world. Confidence in the power of education and science is reflected in the writings of the time.[33] Deafness as a concern of both education and science was given considerable attention. More people than ever before were interested in deafness and its problems, with a plethora of books written on the subject. In 1620, Juan Martin Pablo Bonet published a book on teaching articulation and language, a manual alphabet, and sign language for deaf people entitled *Reducción de las Letras y Arte para Enseñar a Hablar los Mudos*.[34] There is some controversy as to the origin of ideas and methods espoused in the book. His techniques resemble those of other great teachers, yet he claims them for his own. Nevertheless, this was the first book of its kind to be published.[35]

The medical field was also making its contribution to the understanding of the nature of deafness. This new surge of interest is aptly illustrated by the work of a Swedish physician, Felix Platter. Some of Platter's contributions were detailed anatomical drawings of the bones of the ear, comments on the phenomenon of the conduction of sound through the osseous structures in the head, and his observation that the tinnitus (noises in the ear) which many deaf people experience contributed to their confusion in hearing. Platter also noted that, while those who were deaf from birth were always mute, people

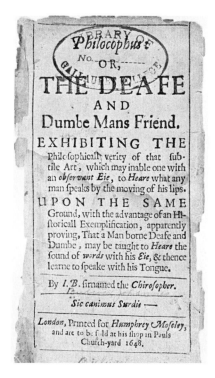

Figure 1. Title page of *Philocophus* or *The Deafe and Dumbe Mans Friend*, by John Bulwer, 1648. Courtesy of Gallaudet College, Washington, D.C.

deafened in life or who could hear even a little could sometimes learn to speak.[36]

Naturally, this new medical interest did not always result in accurate conclusions. One entertaining theory was posed by Anthony Deusing, medical professor at Groningen, the Netherlands. Deusing believed the eustachian tube to be "the 'conduit pipe' by which we heard our own voices with our ears stopped, or music, when we held a stick in our teeth and touched a musical instrument."[37]

Along with the new medical observations concerning deafness, considerable interest was growing in the fundamental nature of language and speech. Although many theorists at this time wrote and published works on language and communica-

Figure 2. Frontispiece to *Chirologia,* or *The Naturall Language of the Hand,* by John Bulwer, 1644. Courtesy of Gallaudet College, Washington, D.C.

tion for those who were deaf, most of the principles were never applied to the actual teaching of deaf children. The publications by John Bulwer are especially noteworthy because they were the first attempts in English to deal at length with deafness and its language implications. *Philocophus* or *The Deafe and Dumbe Mans Friend,* published in 1648, was the first book in English to deal with the subject of lipreading.[38] *Chirologia,* or *The Naturall Language of the Hand,* was another of Bulwer's publications which attempted to analyze manual communication in relation to the application of speech (Figs. 1, 2, and 3).[39, 40]

George Dalgarno was another important theorist of the 1600s

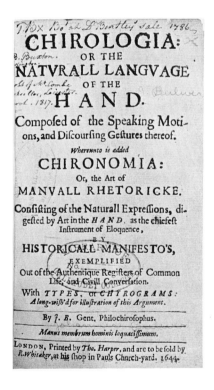

Figure 3. Title page of *Chirologia,* by John Bulwer, 1644. Courtesy of Gallaudet College, Washington, D.C.

who was greatly concerned with technical problems involved in the teaching of language. His work helped lay the foundation for a study essential to the education of deaf children. In 1680, he published *Didascalocophus* or *The Deaf and Dumb Mans Tutor* (Fig. 4).[41] He believed that all signs, vocal or written, were equal though arbitrary.[42] However, like John Bulwer, Dalgarno did not attempt to put his theories into practice, and little notice was taken of his work during his lifetime.[43]

Not all the writers on education of the deaf population were language theorists. Two Englishmen who applied their own theories to their teaching of deaf pupils were John Wallis and William Holder, both born in 1616.[44]

John Wallis' first deaf student was named Daniel Whaley.

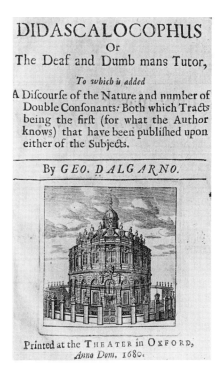

Figure 4. Title page of *Didascalocophus*, by George Dalgarno, 1680. Courtesy of Gallaudet College, Washington, D.C.

Whaley, twenty-five years old, had been deaf since the age of five. After the illness which caused his deafness, he also gradually lost his speech. From communications later published in technical journals of the day, a guide to the technique Wallis employed in teaching Whaley and subsequent students is given.[45]

Wallis began by making use of the gestures Whaley had already developed for communication. Then he proceeded to teach the written alphabet, followed by a manual alphabet. Articulation was taught separately. For the teaching of language, Wallis arranged grammatical steps in logical order, covering classes of nouns, parts of speech, and syntax. The student kept his own homemade dictionary and grammar book along the way.[46] Wallis appears to have been successful in teaching Whaley to speak intelligibly and to write the English language.[47] However, with later students he dropped the teaching of articulation, as he found it not worth the time and effort.[48]

Meanwhile, in 1659, William Holder, the Rector of Bletchington, was requested to teach a deaf child named Alexander Popham. From this experience he was inspired to write the book *Elements of Speech* (Fig. 5), in which he analyzed the positions of speech organs in the pronunciation of various speech elements. Holder arranged the sounds in order of presentation which he suggested for teaching these sounds to deaf children. The sounds were first taught individually, then in syllables, and finally in words associated with the objects they represented. He reportedly used a tongue-shaped leather thong to show a student how to place his tongue.[49]

Unfortunately, after three years of study, young Popham seemed little improved and was able to pronounce only a few words. Descriptions of the boy suggest that he suffered from more than a hearing loss. Discouraged at the slow rate of progress, the boy's mother sent Popham to John Wallis for instruction. Although Wallis later claimed success with Popham, there is no evidence to support this claim.[50]

Not surprisingly, Holder and Wallis entered into a dispute. They were in disagreement as to who was the first teacher to describe a successful method for teaching deaf persons; each

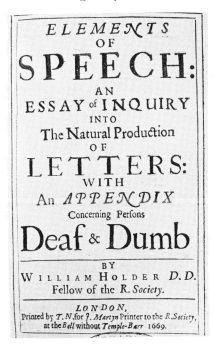

Figure 5. Title page of *Elements of Speech*, by William Holder, 1669. Courtesy of Gallaudet College, Washington, D.C.

claimed the honor for himself.[51] In the end, it was perhaps in this argument that both Holder and Wallis made their most lasting "contribution" to the education of the deaf. As Kenneth Hodgson noted in his book, *The Deaf and Their Problems*, "Whaley and Popham were the first two (deaf) children in England to be taught, Wallis and Holder the first two teachers, as far as we know, and theirs the first quarrel. This petty tendency was unfortunately to remain a feature of the work."[52]

The quarrel between Wallis and Holder did have one beneficial effect; it served to arouse public interest in the problems of deafness to a greater degree than ever before.[53]

During the 1600s in Germany, a Belgian chemist, F. M. Van Helmont, had published an extraordinary book (1667) entitled *Alphabeti vere naturalis Hebraici brevissima delineatio* (a brief description of the actual, natural Hebrew alphabet). During

this period in history, many learned persons were actively engaged in speculation of various cabalistic doctrines. Van Helmont was apparently one such person. The doctrine held that
reality was contained within the configuration of the Hebrew
alphabet and that the letters held the ultimate secrets of the
cosmos. The universe was believed to be composed of thirty-
two elements that corresponded to the first ten numbers and
twenty-two letters of the alphabet.[54] Van Helmont postulated in
his book that the Hebrew language was most natural to man
and "that the shape and character of each letter of the alphabet
conformed to the position and relations of the several speech
organs concerned in its production."[56] The book contained a
series of copperplate engravings in which he depicted a cross

Figure 6. Frontispiece of Van Helmont's book, *Alphabetum Naturae*, 1667.
The picture illustrates the scientist at work, measuring with calipers the
position of the speech organs. Courtesy of Gallaudet College, Washington,
D.C.

section of a person's head revealing the speech organs that corresponded to the Hebrew letter involved (Figs. 6 and 7).

By the end of the seventeenth century, the teaching of deaf children was rapidly becoming a profession in many European countries.

EIGHTEENTH CENTURY

It was in the beginning of the eighteenth century that the first permanent schools for deaf children were established.[57] Although these first schools were of great value to the pupils, they were of equal importance to educators because they provided opportunities for observing and working with deaf persons on a large scale.[58]

Abbé Charles Michel de l'Épée (1712-1789) of Paris founded the first free school for deaf pupils. He lived much of his life as an obscure priest, but like Pedro Ponce de Leon he was concerned with the salvation of deaf persons. He was the first to make the education of deaf children available to the poor as well as the wealthy (Fig. 8).[59] Aside from being a school for those deaf children, de l'Épée's establishment was also a home. He lived with his pupils, taking care of their physical needs as well as their education, all at his expense.[60]

He considered sign language to be a "mother tongue" for those who were deaf[61] and saw no reason to teach them articulation.[62] He hoped to expand sign language so that it could be used to express abstract thought and began this project by writing a dictionary and grammar of signs.[63] The single-handed alphabet he used was derived from that proposed by Juan Pablo Bonet (1620). Later this revised system was brought to the United States, where its use is continued today.[64]

Since Abbé de l'Épée was educating deaf persons for religious salvation, he was concerned that as many people as possible receive schooling. For this reason, he was eager to train teachers and to share his knowledge.[65]

By the time of his death in 1789 at the age of 77, Abbé de

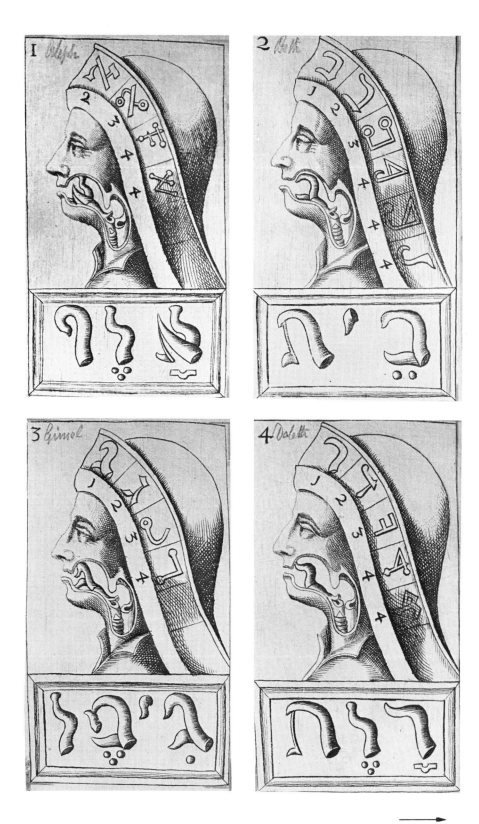

Figure 8. Abbé Charles Michel de l'Épée (1712-1789). Courtesy of Gallaudet College, Washington, D.C.

Figure 7. (1-4) Illustrations from Van Helmont's *Alphabetum Hebraici*. Note position of the speech organs as they correspond to the four letters of the Hebrew alphabet. (1) the *ah* as in the Hebrew letter *aleph*. (2) The *b* sound, as in the letter *bet*. (3) The *g* sound corresponds to the letter *gimel*. (4) The *d* sound, as in the Hebrew letter *daleth*. Courtesy of Gallaudet College, Washington, D.C.

l'Épée was famous in all of Europe for his work with persons who were deaf and mute.[66] A former student of his, Roch Ambroise Cucurron Sicard (Fig. 9), was appointed the new director of the school. In 1790, the institution was moved to the Celestine convent and was given a government grant for the support of the work.[67] By the time of Sicard's death in 1822, the *silent method* of teaching deaf pupils by signs instead of speech was known as the *French method*.[68]

While de l'Épée was establishing the silent method in France, Samuel Heinicke (Fig. 10) was practicing his (the *German*) oral method. In his approach, Heinicke relied on speech and speechreading as the method of communication.[69] In his work, Heinicke was much influenced by the earlier writings of the Swiss physician Johann C. Amman (1692), who is regarded by many as the father of the pure oral system.[70]

In his own time, Heinicke did not gain wide support, despite his accomplishments, because he wrote very little. Today, however, his work serves as the basis of modern oral teaching.[71]

L'ABBÉ SICARD,
Successeur de l'abbé de l'Épée,
mort en 1822, agé de 80 ans.

Figure 9. Abbé Roch Ambroise Cucurron Sicard (1742-1822). Courtesy of Gallaudet College, Washington, D.C.t260

Samuel Heinicke.

Figure 10. Samuel Heinicke (1729-1790). Courtesy of Gallaudet College, Washington, D.C.

Following the lead of de l'Épée and Heinicke, other schools for deaf children were established throughout Europe. The first school for deaf children in Italy was opened in 1784 in Rome by Abba Silvestri, a former student of de l'Épée.[72] Henry Daniel Guyot (1753-1828) founded the Groningen Institution for Deaf-Mutes in the Netherlands. Although influenced by de l'Épée, Guyot used the *old Dutch* or mixed method in his school.[73] In

England, Thomas Braidwood started another school for deaf pupils. For many years, his methods were kept a family secret, but upon his death, they were revealed as being largely oral, based on the system of Wallis.[74] Braidwood, however, recommended the use of the two-handed alphabet (still in use in England today) until oral language could be developed.[75]

SCHOOLS FOR DEAF CHILDREN IN AMERICA — THE NINETEENTH CENTURY

The first permanent school for deaf children in the United States to become a free public school was founded in Hartford, Connecticut, by a minister named Thomas Hopkins Gallaudet.[76] Before the founding of this school in Connecticut, most deaf children of wealthy parents in North America were sent to England for their education.[77] One parent instrumental in changing this situation was Dr. Mason F. Cogswell, the father of a deaf girl named Alice. It was his hope that a school for deaf children would someday be established in the United States.[78,79]

In 1812, at the request of Dr. Cogswell, a survey was taken which showed there were eighty-four "deaf-and-dumb" persons residing in the state of Connecticut. It was estimated that there were probably 400 such persons in New England, and 2,000 throughout the United States. Using this information, in 1815 Dr. Cogswell convinced influential friends of the need for establishing a school for deaf children in America,[80,81] and enough money was soon raised to send a teacher to Europe to study the technique of educating deaf youngsters.[82,83]

During the winter of 1814-1815, Thomas Hopkins Gallaudet (Fig. 11), a young minister, was confined to his home in Hartford, Connecticut, due to illness. During his recovery, he became interested in teaching the deaf child of one of his neighbors; the neighbor was Dr. Mason J. Cogswell, and the child was little Alice.[84] When the money was raised in 1815 to enable a teacher of deaf children to travel to England for study, the position was offered to Thomas Gallaudet. Gallaudet's skills and dedication were apparent from the keen interest he

Figure 11. Thomas Hopkins Gallaudet (1787-1851). Courtesy of Gallaudet College, Washington, D.C.

had shown while working with Alice Cogswell (Fig. 12).[85]

On May 25, 1815, Gallaudet sailed to England intending to study the Braidwood oral method. He was, however, unable to

Figure 12. Statue of Thomas Hopkins Gallaudet and Alice Cogswell. Courtesy of The American School for the Deaf, West Hartford, Connecticut.

make satisfactory arrangements with the Braidwoods and traveled instead to Paris where he studied the manual methods of the Abbé Sicard.[86,87] Gallaudet returned to the United States in the summer of 1816, accompanied by Laurent Clerc, a deaf man who would become the first deaf teacher of deaf children in the United States.[88,89] In introducing Clerc to the Bishop of Boston, the Abbé Sicard wrote: "I would fain regard him as the Apostle to the deaf-mutes of the New World."[90] These words are inscribed on Clerc's monument.[91]

In October, 1816, the legislature of Connecticut appropriated money for a school for deaf children, and a large amount of money for a school was also received through private donations.[92] On April 15, 1817, the first permanent school for deaf students in the United States opened in Hartford, Connecticut, with seven pupils.[93] Within a year, the number of pupils grew to thirty-three.[94] The school was first named the Connecticut Asylum for the Education and Instruction of Deaf and Dumb Persons. In 1819, the name was changed to the American Asylum of the Deaf at Hartford, for the Education and Instruction of the Deaf and Dumb. Today, the school is known as the American School for the Deaf (Fig. 13).[95]

Two years after the founding of the American School for the Deaf, Laurent Clerc went to Washington, D.C., to obtain federal help for the school. He was received with honor by President James Monroe and the Speaker of the House of Representatives, Henry Clay.[96] Soon other states began following Connecticut's example in establishing schools for deaf children. Most of these early schools employed the manual system established by Gallaudet at Hartford, but another method, the oral system, was soon to become popular.[97]

In 1843, Horace Mann (1796-1859) visited schools for deaf children in Europe, where he was most impressed by the German and English oral methods. Upon his return to America, he published a report advocating the use of the oral system.

Another advocate of the oral method was Samuel Gridley Howe (1801-1876) of the Perkins Institute for the Blind. One day Howe was approached by Gardiner Hubbard, the father of

Figure 13. The American School for the Deaf at West Hartford, Connecticut. Courtesy of Gallaudet College, Washington, D.C.

a young deaf girl. Hubbard was seeking advice on the ways to educate his daughter, Mabel. Howe advised him to have Mabel tutored along with hearing children, without the use of manual signs. Hubbard had been tireless in his efforts to find what he felt was the best educational approach available for his daughter. He had been repulsed by the advice previously given him regarding the current methodologies of educating deaf children practiced at Hartford[98] and sought an alternative approach.

As a result of Horace Mann's report advocating the use of the oral system, other parents of deaf children began to demand that speech be taught to their children.[99] The school at Hartford opposed these early attempts to open an oral school most vigorously.[100]

Then, in 1866, a local school teacher at Chelmesford, Massachusetts, Harriet Rogers, placed the following advertisement in an attempt to start an oral program:

> Miss Rogers proposes to take a few deaf-mutes as pupils for
> instruction in articulation and reading from the lips, without
> the use of signs or the finger alphabet. The number is limited
> to seven, two of whom are already engaged.[101]

One year later, Miss Rogers's class had obtained the number
of pupils she desired. That same year the philanthropist John
Clarke offered $50,000 if a school could be established in North-
ampton, Massachusetts. Miss Rogers's class was subsequently
moved to Northampton and later became known as the Clarke
School for the Deaf.

Another oral school started in 1867 also resulted from a private class; the New York Institution for the Improved Instruction of Deaf-Mutes.[102]

The first nonresidential school for deaf children was the
School for Deaf-Mutes established in Boston in 1869.[103,104] The
name of the school was later changed to the Horace Mann
School.[105,106] It was quickly followed by the opening of other
day schools and classes throughout the country.[107]

. A discussion of the education of deaf children in nineteenth-
century America would not be complete without mention of
Alexander Graham Bell (Fig. 14). Bell's mother was deaf; his
father, Alexander Melville Bell (1819-1905), was a teacher of
diction and elocution at Edinburgh, Scotland and was interested in the concept of a universal language.[108] As a result of
this interest, he developed a phonetic alphabet system he called
Visible Speech (Fig. 15).[109,110] Alexander Graham Bell became
interested in the communication problems of deaf persons
largely as a result of his father's Visible Speech system. In 1871,
young Bell went to Boston where he taught instructors at the
Horace Mann School for the Deaf to use Visible Speech with
their students.[111] While living in Boston, Bell began to tutor
Mabel Hubbard, whom he later married.[112] As C. Joseph Giangreco and Marianne Ranson Giangreco so aptly indicated,
"Bell's mother was deaf; Bell taught the deaf and then took
Mabel Hubbard as his wife. It is thus understandable that Bell
felt a very close tie to the education of the deaf and influenced
it both in word and deed."[113]

Figure 14. Alexander Graham Bell (1847-1922). Courtesy of Gallaudet College, Washington, D.C.

ILLUSTRATION OF "VISIBLE SPEECH"

Bᴀsɪs ᴏꜰ Sʏᴍʙᴏʟs

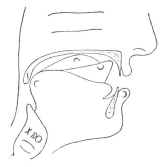

BASIS FOR CONSONANT SYMBOLS

C Back of Tongue.
∩ Top " "
U Point " "
Ɔ Lips.

ʃ Nasal passage open.
X Glottis closed.
I " vocalizing.
O " open (aspirate).

◊ Throat aspirate (whisper).

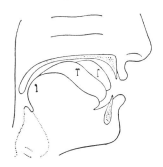

BASIS FOR VOWEL SYMBOLS

On left   side of line,   (ꟾ) back of mouth.
On right   "   "   (ꟾ) front "   "
On both sides   "   (ꟾ) mixed, back and front.
At top   "   (ꟾ) high.
At bottom   "   (ꟾ) low.
At both ends   "   (ꟾ) mid elevation.

A cross bar on a line denotes rounding or contraction of the lips. A point, or a hook, on a straight line denotes the vowel positions of the tongue.

Figure 15. Illustration of *Visible Speech*. From Harry Best, *Deafness and the Deaf in the United States*, 1943. Courtesy of Macmillan Publishing Company, Inc., New York, New York.

Although the Visible Speech system eventually proved to be impractical for use with young deaf pupils,[114] Bell's interest in the education of deaf children continued.

It was Bell's concern for deaf persons which led to his invention of the telephone. Although it is not generally known, the telephone was largely the result of experiments Bell was conducting for development of an instrument to help deaf people learn to speak.[115] The telephone ultimately proved to be of benefit to the deaf population, since it was the telephone-type earphone which was later used in hearing aids.[116]

In 1887, Bell and his father established the Volta Bureau[117,118] "for the increase and diffusion of knowledge relating to the deaf."[119] Bell also improved the United States Census in 1890, so that the deaf population could be more accurately counted, and it is through his efforts that the term *deaf* was officially substituted for *deaf-mute*.[120]

In 1857, a small private school for deaf children opened in Washington, D.C.[121,122] This institution was named the Kendall School,[123] after its founder Amos Kendall (Fig. 16), the postmaster general of the United States.[124,125] The principal was Edward Miner Gallaudet (1837-1919), the youngest son of Thomas Hopkins Gallaudet. Seven years later, Kendall School became the Columbia Institution for the Deaf.[126,127] Edward Miner Gallaudet had a dream of starting a college for deaf scholars, and he sought to see that dream become a reality. In 1864, President Abraham Lincoln signed an act of Congress that established the school as the first college for deaf students in America, with Edward Miner Gallaudet as its first president. In 1894, the Institution was renamed Gallaudet College in memory of Thomas Hopkins Gallaudet (Fig. 17).[128,129] The preparatory department was named Kendall School after the original benefactor, Amos Kendall.[130] It was at Gallaudet College that the first training center for teachers of deaf children was established in 1891.[131] This was followed by another training center at the Clarke School for the Deaf in Northampton in 1892.[132]

Figure 16. Amos Kendall (1789-1869). Courtesy of Gallaudet College, Washington, D.C.

THE CONTROVERSY EMERGES

Throughout the nineteenth century in America, educators of

Figure 17. College Hall of Gallaudet College. Courtesy of Gallaudet College, Washington, D.C.

deaf children disagreed over the question of methodology (*see* Chap. 3). This controversy, referred to by many as the "one hundred years' war,"[133] continues unabated to this day. It is to a large extent an "empty controversy"[134] filled with misunderstanding, emotionalism, and imprecise terminology. It is not an "old controversy" because it is very much alive today and merits our attention.[135]

As noted previously, the first school for deaf children in Hartford, Connecticut, followed a manual philosophy. It was not until fifty years later in 1867 that the first oral residential schools for deaf children were opened.

In 1868, the question of methodology was discussed at a conference held in Washington, D.C., with representatives from the schools for deaf children in the United States. The resolution of the conference was "In the opinion of this conference it is the duty of all institutions for the deaf and dumb to provide adequate means of imparting instruction in articulation and lipreading to such of their pupils as may be able to profit in exercises of this nature."[136]

A worldwide conference for educators of deaf students was held twelve years later in Milan, Italy, in 1880. The answer to the oral-manual controversy was that "considering the incontestable superiority of articulation over signs in restoring the deaf-mute to Society and giving him a fuller knowledge of language, the Conference declares that the oral method should be preferred to that of signs in the education of the deaf."[137]

In 1885, a commission was created in England to investigate educational methodologies for deaf pupils, so that provision could be made for the education of these children in the United Kingdom. After 116 sittings and the testimony of forty-three experts, including Edward Miner Gallaudet and Alexander Graham Bell, the commission offered a compromising resolution, which declared in part,

> that every child who is deaf should have full opportunity of being educated in the pure oral system. In all schools which receive Government grants, whether conducted on the oral, sign and manual, or combined systems, all children should be, for the first year at least, instructed on the oral system and after the first year they should be taught to speak and lip-read on the pure oral system, unless they are physically or mentally disqualified, in which case, with the consent of the parents, they should be either removed from the oral department of the school or taught elsewhere on the sign and manual system.[138]*

By the end of the nineteenth century, *oralism* was the officially preferred method of instruction for deaf children.

THE TWENTIETH CENTURY

The twentieth century marked the opening of a new era for those who were deaf, as well as those who were hard of hearing; the era of electrical amplification. For centuries, sound-amplification devices available to deaf persons had been limited to ear trumpets and conversation tubes.[139] These sound-collecting devices were often imaginatively designed and could amplify sound by as much as 20 decibels.[140] Such equipment worked on the principle of gathering sound waves and channeling them into the ear.[141] Throughout history an imaginative assortment of various devices were employed to aid hearing. One early device is the soundtrumpet described by Athanasius Kircher, S.J., in 1673 in his volume *Phonurgia Nova*.[142] This

---

*An interesting aside is that two of the commission members would not sanction the recommendation "because the oral method was not recommended exclusively, while two others dissented for the reason that it was deemed by them too strong an endorsement of that method."

simple device employed an elliptical tube through which the voice of the speaker entered at one end and the listener placed his ear at the other end to receive the sound transmission.[143]

Other early conical tubes as described by Kircher (*Phonurgia,* 1713) were quite popular. Sound-amplification devices became improved in time and resulted in smaller and more elaborate models.

One interesting model was an elegantly fashioned ram's horn. It was polished to a high finish and adorned with silver and ivory. The listener placed the smaller end to his ear and held the instrument toward the speaker. This instrument was very popular in nineteenth-century England.[144] Other devices were shaped like shells, snails, and trumpets, and many were designed to be concealed by the hair.

There is some controversy as to who actually produced the first electronic hearing aid. Some sources credit Ferdinand Alt, an assistant in the Politzer Clinic of Venice, in 1900. Others claim the first wearable electric hearing aid was made in 1902, by Miller Reese Hutchinson of Mobile, Alabama. However, regardless of the originator, by 1920 the Marconi Company was marketing the first valve amplifier hearing aids.

The 1920s also saw the inclusion of auditory training into the educational programs of many schools for deaf children. Much of the credit for the advancement of auditory training in the American schools for deaf youngsters must be attributed to Max Goldstein, M.D. (Fig. 18).[145] Goldstein, a noted otologist in the United States, strongly advocated the importance of residual hearing.[146] In 1914, he established the Central Institute for the Deaf in Saint Louis, Missouri. This was to be a private oral school[147] where Goldstein incorporated his *acoustic method,* wherein the child's residual hearing is utilized and developed to the greatest possible extent.[148]

Because of Goldstein's success and the development of ever-more-sophisticated sound-amplification devices, auditory training programs spread throughout the special schools for deaf children.

In 1926, the acoustic engineers of the Bell Telephone Laboratory developed the audiometer.[149] With this invention, the ability to discover and analyze an individual's hearing loss was

Figure 18. Dr. Max Goldstein (1870-1941). Noted otologist and founder of the Central Institute of the Deaf in St. Louis, Missouri. Courtesy of the Central Institute for the Deaf, St. Louis, Missouri.

greatly improved.

Medical science in the twentieth century gave the world middle and inner ear operations to alleviate many types of hearing loss, and antibiotics were discovered to effectively combat many of the childhood diseases that had sometimes resulted in deafness.[150] Cochlear implants* and other seemingly

---

*A surgical procedure that bypasses the outer and middle ear entirely to stimulate the hair cells in the inner ear.

miraculous operations led some to believe that there might soon be no need for special residential schools for deaf children. Such optimism may have been justified in the light of scientific progress, modern technology, and the general history of remarkable achievements that, a few decades ago, would have been considered the "stuff of which dreams are made." It may not have been too radical a belief, considering the acceleration of progress, that the disability of deafness could soon be conquered.

REFERENCES

1. Ruth E. Bender, *The Conquest of Deafness* (Cleveland: Press of Western Reserve University, 1970), p. 18.
2. Plutarch, "Growing Up in Sparta." In Margaret Gillett (ed.), *Readings in the History of Education* (Toronto: McGraw-Hill Company of Canada, 1969), p. 29.
3. Bender, pp. 22-23.
4. Kenneth W. Hodgson, *The Deaf and Their Problems: A Study In Special Education* (New York: Philosophical Library, 1954), p. 69.
5. Leviticus, 19:14.
6. Hodgson, p. 71.
7. *Ibid.*
8. *Ibid.*, pp. 71-72.
9. *Ibid.*, p. 72.
10. Bender, p. 21.
11. *Ibid.*, p. 23.
12. Hodgson, p. 60.
13. *Ibid.*, p. 61.
14. Bender, p. 21.
15. *Ibid.*
16. Hodgson, p. 62.
17. *Ibid.*, p. 72.
18. *Ibid.*, pp. 72-73.
19. *Ibid.*, p. 73.
20. *Ibid.*
21. *Ibid.*
22. *Ibid.*
23. Bender, p. 32.
24. *Ibid.*, p. 33.
25. Edna S. Levine, *Youth in a Soundless World; A Search for Personality* (New York: New York University Press, 1956), p. 18.
26. Hodgson, p. 74.

27. *Ibid.*, p. 84.
28. *Ibid.*
29. *Ibid.*, p. 85.
30. Bender, p. 41.
31. *Ibid.*, p. 48.
32. *Ibid.*, pp. 47-48.
33. *Ibid.*, p. 49.
34. *Ibid.*, p. 43.
35. Harry Best, *Deafness and the Deaf in the United States* (New York: Macmillan Company, 1943), p. 376.
36. Bender, p. 51.
37. *Ibid.*, pp. 53-54.
38. Max A. Goldstein, *Problems of the Deaf* (St. Louis: Laryngoscope Press, 1933), p. 20.
39. *Ibid.*
40. Bender, p. 54.
41. Hodgson, pp. 91-92.
42. *Ibid.*, p. 92.
43. Bender, p. 58.
44. *Ibid.*, p. 59.
45. *Ibid.*, p. 60.
46. *Ibid.*
47. *Ibid.*
48. *Ibid.*, pp. 60-61.
49. *Ibid.*, pp. 61-62.
50. *Ibid.*, p. 63.
51. *Ibid.*
52. Hodgson, p. 101.
53. *Ibid.*, p. 103.
54. R. J. Zwi Werblowsky, "Cabala." In Richard Cavendish (ed.), *Man, Myth & Magic,* (New York: Marshal Cavendish Corporation, 1970), vol. 3, p. 383.
55. *Ibid.*, p. 387.
56. Goldstein, p. 26.
57. Bender, p. 129.
58. Edna S. Levine, *Youth in a Soundless World: A Search for Personality* (New York: New York University Press, 1956), p. 19.
59. Bender, p. 79.
60. *Ibid.*, p. 85.
61. *Ibid.*, p. 81.
62. *Ibid.*
63. *Ibid.*, pp. 81-82.
64. Best, p. 518.
65. Bender, p. 81.
66. *Ibid.*, p. 86.

67. *Ibid.*, pp. 86-87.

68. *Ibid.*, p. 93.

69. John J. O'Neill and Herbert J. Oyer, *Visual Communication For the Hard of Hearing* (Englewood Cliffs, New Jersey: Prentice-Hall, 1961), p. 12.

70. Henry Winter Syle, *A Retrospect of the Education of the Deaf on the Occasion of the Clerc Centennial Commemoration, December 28, 1885* (Philadelphia: Wm. R. Cullingworth, 1886), p. 14.

71. Hodgson, p. 138.

72. Bender, p. 99.

73. *Ibid.*, p. 109.

74. Best, p. 381.

75. Bender, p. 117.

76. Best, p. 389.

77. Bender, p. 120.

78. *Ibid.*, p. 123.

79. Richard G. Brill, *The Education of the Deaf* (Washington, D.C.: Gallaudet College Press, 1974), p. 8.

80. Bender pp. 123-124.

81. Brill, p. 8.

82. Bender, p. 124.

83. Brill, p. 8.

84. *Ibid.*

85. Bender, p. 124.

86. *Ibid.*, p. 126.

87. Brill, p. 9.

88. *Ibid.*

89. Bender, p. 126.

90. Syle, p. 25.

91. *Ibid.*

92. Bender, p. 126.

93. *Ibid.*

94. Brill, p. 9.

95. *Ibid.*

96. Syle, p. 25.

97. Bender, p. 148.

98. C. Joseph Giangreco and Marianne Ranson Giangreco, *The Education of the Hearing Impaired* (Springfield, Illinois: Charles C Thomas, Publisher, 1970), p. 25.

99. Bender, pp. 148-149.

100. *Ibid.*, p. 150.

101. Gardiner G. Hubbard, *The Story of the Rise of the Oral Method in America As Told in the Writings of the Late Hon. Gardiner G. Hubbard* (Washington, D.C.: Press of W. F. Roberts, 1898), p. 28.

102. Bender, p. 151.

103. Bender, p. 149.
104. Brill, p. 11.
105. Bender, p. 149.
106. Brill, p. 11.
107. Best, p. 454.
108. Bender, p. 152.
109. *Ibid.*
110. Best, pp. 545-546.
111. George W. Fellendorf, "75 Years of Excitement." *Volta Review, 78,* 2:100.
112. Bender, p. 157.
113. Giangreco, p. 26.
114. Bender, p. 156.
115. Kenneth W. Berger, "From Telephone to Electric Hearing Aid." *Volta Review, 78,* 2:83-84.
116. Berger, pp. 83-89.
117. *Ibid.,* p. 84.
118. Bender, p. 159.
119. Fellendorf, p. 100.
120. Bender, p. 159.
121. *Ibid.*
122. Bender, p. 160.
123. Hodgson, p. 220.
124. *Ibid.,* p. 221.
125. Bender, p. 160.
126. Hodgson, p. 220.
127. Bender, p. 160.
128. Hodgson, p. 221.
129. Bender, p. 160.
130. Hodgson, p. 221.
131. Brill, p. 47.
132. *Ibid.*
133. Richard G. Brill, "Total Communication as A Basis of Educating Prelingually Deaf Children." In *Communication Symposium* (Frederick, Maryland: Maryland School for the Deaf, 1970), p. 7.
134. David M. Denton, "Remarks in Support of A System of Total Communication for Deaf Children." In *Communication Symposium* (Frederick, Maryland: Maryland School for the Deaf, 1970), p. 5.
135. Eugene Mindel, "Studies on the Deaf Child." In R. G. Grinker (ed.), *Psychiatric Diagnosis, Therapy and Research on the Psychotic Deaf,* Final Report, Grant #RD-2407-S, Social Rehabiliation Service, U.S. Department of Health, Education, and Welfare. (Washington, D.C.: U.S. Government Printing Office, 1969), p. 78.
136. Hodgson, pp. 282-283.
137. *Ibid.,* p. 243.
138. Joseph Claybaugh Gordon, *Notes and Observations Upon the*

Education of the Deaf (Washington, D.C.: Volta Bureau, 1892), p. xvi.
139. Bender, p. 178.
140. Hodgson, p. 302.
141. Bender, p. 178.
142. Goldstein, p. 304.
143. *Ibid.*
144. *Ibid.*, p. 325.
145. Herbert J. Oyer, *Auditory Communication for the Hard of Hearing* (Englewood Cliffs, New Jersey: Prentice-Hall, 1966), p. 10.
146. *Ibid.*
147. Bender, p. 171.
148. Edna Simon Levine, *The Psychology of Deafness: Techniques of Appraisal for Rehabilitation* (New York: Columbia University Press, 1960), p. 322.
149. Bender, p. 172.
150. *Ibid.*, pp. 189-190.

— CHAPTER 2 —

BY SIGHT OR SOUND

IN discussion, it is often necessary to pause and define terms germane to the topic. One of the continuing problems in the education of deaf children has been the impreciseness of terminology and a consequent misunderstanding and confusion on the part of educators, parents, and the interested public.

THE CHARACTERISTICS OF SOUND

The decibel (dB) is a unit used to measure hearing loss, a measurement of the physical energy of sound. Loudness is its psychological counterpart.[1] The threshold of hearing is measured as 0 decibels; a whisper is +20 dB; conversation is approximately +60 dB. Beyond an intensity level of +120 dB, pain occurs.[2] Frequency refers to that property which can be measured and is reported as Hertz (Hz). The number of vibrations per second of a sound wave determines the pitch of the heard tone. The intact human auditory mechanism can perceive tones between 15 and 15,000 Hz (cycles per second).[3] For the most part, speech occurs in the narrow range of pitches between 300 and 4,000 cycles per second (Fig. 19).[4]

HEARING AND HEARING LOSS

Hearing capacity may be regarded as "a function of the individual's ability to discriminate and understand the sounds that reach him."[5] When a person's hearing capacity is diminished to the extent that he is unable to hear and understand connected speech, he is said to be deaf.[6] A person with a significant hearing loss who is able to understand connected speech with or without amplification is said to be hard of hearing.[7]

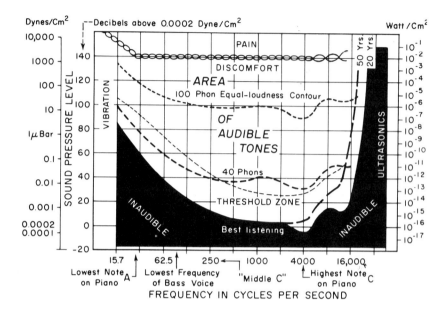

Figure 19. The auditory area. From D. W. Robinson and R. S. Dadson, *Journal of the Acoustical Society of America, 29*:1284-1288, 1957. Courtesy of the American Institute of Physics, New York, New York.

CLASSIFICATIONS OF HEARING IMPAIRMENT

Hearing impairments may be divided into six categories, according to the degree of hearing loss in the speech range measured in decibel units. In considering such a classification, it must be remembered that each child is unique in his response to a hearing loss, and two children with similar decibel losses may function at different levels. Any classification scheme of this sort can serve only as a general guide.*

NORMAL: A 10 to 24 decibel loss is normal. No significant difficulty with faint speech is apparent. A whisper, it might be remembered, is +20 dB.

---

*The divisions in this classification are those suggested by Eugene Mindel, M.D., and McCay Vernon, Ph.D., in their book, *They Grow in Silence*, 1971, published by the National Association of the Deaf, Silver Spring, Maryland.

SLIGHT: A 25 to 39 decibel loss is slight. Such a loss may pass unnoticed or may result in difficulty in hearing faint or distant speech. Such difficulty depends largely on how close the loss is to the 40 dB level, the distance of the child from the sound source, and the quality of the sound.

MILD TO MODERATE: A 40 to 54 decibel loss is mild to moderate. The child generally understands conversational speech if the distance is limited to 3 to 5 feet. Difficulty in hearing is related to such factors as attentiveness of the child, distance from the source of the sound, extraneous noise, and poor articulation or "soft" speech.

MODERATELY SEVERE: A 55 to 69 decibel loss is moderately severe. The sounds must be loud and the distance small for the child to hear. Considerable difficulty arises unless conversation is directed exclusively to the child. It is helpful to remember that conversation is approximately +60 dB.

SEVERE: A 70 to 89 decibel loss is severe. Shouted conversation is probably not heard. With this degree of loss, the child is not able to learn speech by conventional means. Such children are often considered *educationally deaf,* as are some children with a moderately severe hearing loss.

PROFOUND LOSS: Over 90 decibels is profound loss. Occasional loud sounds may be heard, but the child perceives vibrations rather than complete sound patterns.

DEAFNESS: Children with a moderately severe to a severe loss are often on the borderline between the hard of hearing and the deaf. Children with profound losses are considered to be deaf.

For educational purposes, those children who are deaf may be further subdivided into two distinct groups, depending upon the age attained at the onset of their hearing loss.

PRELINGUALLY DEAF: Those children who were born deaf or who became deaf at such an early age (before two or three years of age) that they did not have the opportunity to acquire normal speech and language patterns are prelingually deaf.[8,9]

POSTLINGUALLY DEAF: Children who had relatively normal hearing for at least the first two to three years of life and there-

Total Communication

TABLE I.
HEARING THRESHOLD LEVELS AND IMPACT ON
COMMUNICATION AND LANGUAGE*

Hearing Threshold Levels (ISO)	Probable Impact on Communication and Language	Present-Day Implications for Educational Settings	
		Type†	Probable Need
Level I‡ 26-54 dB	Mild	Full Integration	Most Frequent
		Partial Integration	Frequent
		Self-Contained	Infrequent
Level II 55-69 dB	Moderate	Full Integration	Frequent
		Partial Integration	Most Frequent
		Self-Contained	Infrequent
Level III 70-89 dB	Severe	Full Integration	Infrequent
		Partial Integration	Most Frequent
		Self-Contained	Frequent
Level IV 90 dB and above	Profound	Full Integration	Infrequent
		Partial Integration	Frequent
		Self-Contained	Most Frequent

*From Report of the Ad Hoc Committee to Define Deaf and Hard of Hearing, *American Annals of the Deaf, 120,5*:510, 1975. Courtesy of *American Annals of the Deaf,* Washington, D.C.

†Full integration means total integration into regular classes for hearing students with special services provided under direction of specialists in educational programs for deaf and hard of hearing. *Partial integration means taking all classes in a regular school, some on an integrated basis and some on a self-contained basis. Self-contained* means attending classes exclusively with other deaf and/or hard of hearing classmates in regular schools, special day schools or special residential schools.

‡It is assumed that these decibel scores were obtained by a qualified audiologist using an average of scores within the frequency range commonly considered necessary to process linguistic information.

fore were able to develop normal speech and language patterns are postlingually deaf.[10,11]

Due to advances in medical sciences, deafness as the result of childhood diseases such as measles, mumps, and whooping cough is relatively rare. As a consequence, today the majority of deaf students in schools for deaf youngsters are prelingually deaf,[12] and it is with this group of children that Total Communication as an educational philosophy is primarily concerned.

TERMINOLOGY AND EDUCATIONAL PLACEMENT

The educational requirements and goals of the hard-of-hearing or the pre- or postlingually deaf child are quite different; therefore, such distinctions are helpful. Unfortunately, there are many professionals who place these three categories of children under the single rubric of *hearing impaired*. According to some, this term has the advantage of not having the negative connotation of the term *deaf*.[13] It is an unfortunate vestige from the past that such negativism persists in an enlightened society, yet among certain segments it surely does. The disadvantages of using such a broad term as *hearing impaired* to describe at least three fundamentally different conditions of hearing loss are important. The issue of appropriate educational procedures is confused (*see* Table I), and it can further delay parental acceptance of the fact of deafness in the child.[14]

The handicap of deafness is much like an iceberg. Most people are aware of the obvious consequences of being deaf: an inability to hear sounds and speak intelligibly. As unfortunate as these disadvantages are, a far more serious handicap lurks beneath the surface and is often unnoticed until optimum time for learning various skills is passed. The deaf child is all too often deprived of one of the key ingredients of the developmental process: communication with significant others.[15] Communication is essential to the healthy psychological and cognitive development of an individual.

COMMUNICATION, LANGUAGE, AND SPEECH

Communication, by dictionary definition, is the interchange of thoughts, opinions, or information.[16] The act of communicating involves the ability to understand messages of others (receptive communication) and the ability to adequately express one's own messages in a manner which others are able to understand (expressive communication). Communication is the key ingredient of all social relationships. It grows out of human interactions — and the ways in which others react toward us largely depend upon what and by which manner we communicate.[17]

Language is a tool for communication. In this book, language is defined as a system of arbitrary verbal symbols used in a more or less uniform fashion by a number of people who are thus enabled to communicate intelligibly with one another.[18] Communication involves the ability to utilize an accepted symbol system. Language can be used receptively, expressively, and internally (cognitive thinking).[19]

An important distinction must be made between speech and language. Speech is only one mode of language. Other common modes include writing, printing, fingerspelling, and signing.[20] Also, speech ability does not ensure language knowledge. A child may be able to pronounce a word perfectly, yet have no understanding of the word's meaning.[21]

MANUAL COMMUNICATION

Fingerspelling

Fingerspelling is a system which involves the production on the fingers of one hand (or two hands in the British Empire) of a configuration meant to correspond with a letter of the alphabet. It is literally spelling words with the fingers. There is a different configuration for each of the twenty-six letters of the English alphabet,[22] and these twenty-six configurations comprise what is called the *manual alphabet*. When this system is used simultaneously with speech in an educational setting, it is often referred to as the *Rochester Method.*[23]

Sign Language

Sign language refers to a means of communication where the

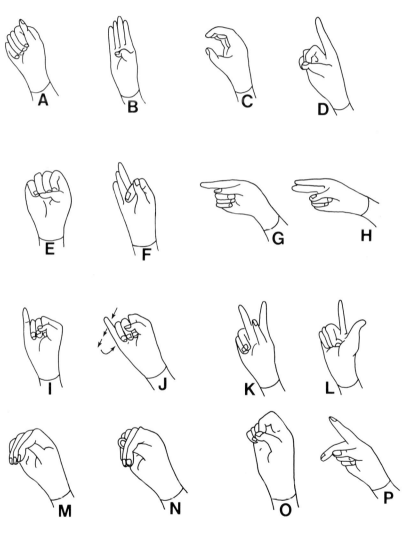

Figure 20. (A and B) The manual alphabet. Illustrated by Cheryl Pahz.

message

> . . . consists of visual patterns, produced by gestures and received by the eye. Each gesture is made by one or both hands, held in specific configuration and at a particular portion of the message-sender's body; the hand or hands are either still or traverse a certain motion for a particular meaning. The configuration of the hand, its placement in front of the body, or the motion itself may be viewed in such a way as to produce signs that are related in meaning.[24]

Historical evidence indicates that different forms of sign language have existed for centuries — an obvious way for deaf

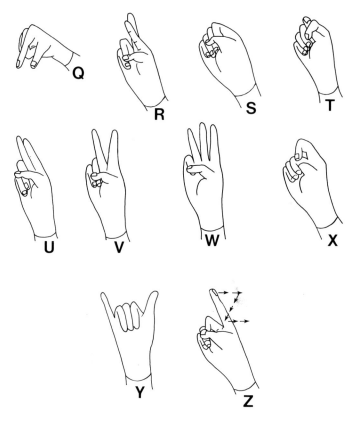

Figure 20B.

persons to cope with the world around them in their efforts to communicate with others. The American Sign Language, as used today, is oftentimes referred to as having descended from the system formulated by Abbé Charles Michel de l'Épée[25] and subsequently refined by teachers of deaf children in the United States, as well as by deaf people themselves.

THE PARAMETERS OF SIGN

Signs are recognized as having four parameters, called *cheremes*. These cheremes are the building blocks of signs, just as phonemes are the basic elements of speech. The four cheremes for signs are (1) configuration, (2) movement, (3) orientation, and (4) place of contact. When these cheremes are combined simultaneously, they form the sign vocabulary.[26]

Today, there are over two thousand formal manual signs. However, this is not to imply that only two thousand concepts or situations can be expressed through signs, since the meaning of a sign is derived from the context in which the individual sign is used.[27]

The *American Sign Language* (ASL) is the basis for most of the new manual systems being developed in America today. ASL is recognized as a formal language, separate and distinct from English, whereas until recently it was usually considered a different English form. Even today, many claim that ASL is a "concrete" language and limited in its capacity to deal with abstraction. It is no more "concrete" than spoken English, has many more idioms, and is capable of dealing with all manner of abstractions. ASL may be supplemented by fingerspelling. When words are fingerspelled, they are English words which are borrowed, just as English borrows words from other languages.

SIGN LANGUAGE SYSTEMS

Sign English (Siglish or *Ameslish)* is an ASL-based system modified to English syntax and word order. Instead of inventing new signs, this system utilizes increased fingerspelling.

Figure 21. (A and B) The plethora of sign systems, as portrayed in *Deaf Spectrum*. Courtesy of *Deaf Spectrum*, Beaverton, Oregon.

Sign English is the standard mode of communication used by most deaf adults in this country who have a knowledge of both English and ASL-based signs.[29]

Manual English refers to the systems which retain many root signs of ASL, while at the same time creating new signs or modifying existing signs to conform to English morophology in a visual mode. There are a number of manual English systems, such as *Signed English, Seeing Essential English, Signing Exact English,* and *Linguistics of Visual English* (Fig. 21 A and B).[30] These new systems have created signs for affixes, verb endings, plurality, articles, and English words which previously had no sign equivalents.[31]

GESTEMIC COMMUNICATION

A final manifestation of manual communication is referred to as *gestemic communication* and does not involve formal language.[32] One type of gestemic communication is *childrenese* which refers to the short-lived signs of deaf children, which can be likened to the hearing child's baby talk.[33] Esoteric signs refer to in-group signs peculiar to a specific school, program discipline, or geographic area. Gestemic communication would also include universal gestures — such as waving "hello" or "goodbye."

REFERENCES

1. Eugene D. Mindel and McCay Vernon, *They Grow in Silence; The Deaf Child and His Family* (Silver Spring, Maryland: National Association of the Deaf, 1971), pp. 33-34.
2. Jack Tompkins, "Sound Generation and Transmission," In Darrell E. Rose (ed.), *Audiological Assessment* (Englewood Cliffs, New Jersey: Prentice-Hall, 1971), p. 12.
3. Edna Simon Levine, *The Psychology of Deafness: Techniques of Appraisal for Rehabilitation* (New York: Columbia University Press, 1960), p. 347.
4. Mindel and Vernon, p. 34
5. *Ibid.*, p. 31.
6. Richard G. Brill, "Total Communication as a Basis of Educating Prelingually Deaf Children." In *Communication Symposium*

(Frederick, Maryland: Maryland School for the Deaf, 1970), p. 7.

7. *Ibid.*

8. *Ibid.*

9. McCay Vernon and Eugene D. Mindel, "Psychological and Psychiatric Aspects of Profound Hearing Loss." In Darrell E. Rose (ed.), *Audiological Assessment.* (Englewood Cliffs, New Jersey: Prentice-Hall, 1971), p. 89.

10. Brill, p. 7.

11. Vernon and Mindel, p. 89.

12. Brill, p. 8.

13. Joseph Rosenstein, "Comments on Panel Presentation from the 1972 Alexander Graham Bell Association National Convention," *Volta Review*, 74, 9:562.

14. Brill, p. 8.

15. Hilde S. Schlesinger and Kathryn P. Meadow, *Sound and Sign; Childhood Deafness and Mental Health* (Berkeley: University of California Press, 1972), p. 1.

16. C. L. Barnhart and Jess Stein (eds.), *The American College Dictionary* (New York: Random House, 1962), p. 244.

17. Social Psychology: *Explorations in Understanding* (Del Mar, California: Communications, Research, and Machines, 1974), p. 83.

18. Barnhart and Stein, p. 685.

19. Brill, p. 9.

20. *Ibid.*

21. *Ibid.*

22. Mervin D. Garretson, "Total Communication," *Volta Review*, 78, 4:93.

23. *Ibid.*

24. Schlesinger and Meadow, p. 31.

25. Harry Best, *Deafness and the Deaf in the United States* (New York: Macmillan Company, 1943), p. 518.

26. Garretson, p. 91.

27. Mindel and Vernon, p. 66.

28. Garretson, p. 91.

29. *Ibid.*

30. *Ibid.*

31. *Ibid.*

32. *Ibid.*, pp. 91-92.

33. *Ibid.*, p. 92.

34. *Ibid.*, p. 93.

CHAPTER 3

SYSTEMS OF INSTRUCTION

PRIOR to the emergence of the philosophy of Total Communication in the 1960s, there were two primary systems of educating deaf children. These were referred to as the *oral* and *combined systems*. With some degree of modification, they have continued to survive. Due to differing interpretations of what constitutes the mechanics of these methods, there has generally been a great deal of confusion and lack of agreement concerning their definitions.[1]

THE MANUAL SYSTEM

As was reported earlier, a system of manual signs for teaching the deaf, based on Parisian sign language, was developed by Abbé Charles Michel de l'Épée. The system was later further developed by his successor, Abbé Sicard. The Abbé de l'Épée labeled his signs "methodical," and they were intended primarily for instructional purposes rather than colloquial discourse.[2] The system was also complicated by additional signs intended to convey language usage to pupils of the school in which the system was used.

Because the system did not lend itself well to normal discourse, apparently it was gradually refined to incorporate more "natural" signs developed largely from pantomime. In France, the person largely responsible for this transition was Saint Sernin, a teacher of deaf children who espoused a more natural sign language that should grow from deaf people's usage. In the United States, vestiges of the methodical system lingered longer than on the Continent but gradually evolved into a more "natural" American sign language.

In the early days of instructing deaf pupils, the manual method excluded any form of articulation training. Simply put, such training was considered to be a waste of time. In 1867, the principal of the American School at Hartford commented to a Joint Special Committee of the Massachusetts Legislature,

> The attempt to teach articulation has never been a part of the regular system of instruction of the deaf and dumb, and I hope never will be. We can give them a measure of vocalization, imperfect, to be sure, we can teach some of them to pronounce, parrot-like, words something in the way we do, but we cannot make them (the deaf-born) understand the use of vocal language, with its articulation, its emphasis, its point. It has never been done; it never can be done.[4]

The personnel of the early established schools were not favorably inclined toward those who advocated the teaching of speech, and they generally attempted to thwart the oralists' efforts. But as Mabel Gardiner Bell points out in the posthumous collection of her father's writings, those early educators soon changed their position. Probably it was because of the concern of such notables as Horace Mann, Dr. S. G. Howe, and Gardiner G. Hubbard and the influence they had on the parents of deaf children that gave impetus for the schools' change of philosophy. By 1898, the teaching of articulation had been included in the manual methodology, as indicated by the principal's report of Job Williams.

> The aim of all school instruction should be to aid the pupil to master the English language in order that he may have easy communication with the hearing world about him through the English language, by spoken English in all cases where possible, but when that proves impossible, by written or spelled English.
>
> Even a small degree of speech is valuable. Teach speech, speech, speech by all means, and to the fullest degree, and use it whenever practicable, in school and out of school. Encourage it at all times, and let non-English means of communication be discouraged wherever the English language will answer equally well. English either spoken, written or spelled, is, in the main, the language of our school exercises.[5]

Apparently, however, such intense sentiment did not prevail for very long. According to the 1914 *American Annals of the Deaf* regarding the manual method of instruction,

Signs, the manual alphabet, and writing are the chief means used in the instruction of the pupils, and the principal objects aimed at are mental development and facility in the comprehension and use of written language. The degree of relative importance given to these three means varies in different schools; but it is a difference only in degree, and the end aimed at is the same in all.[6]

It should be emphasized that not since the very earliest days of instruction did any educator advocate teaching deaf children by *manual means only.* The addition of speech teaching and similar activities would lead to the manual method becoming labeled the *combined method.*

THE ORAL SYSTEM

Oralism refers to a method of instruction which has as its goals the development of oral speech, as well as written language and mental abilities. The techniques used to accomplish these aims are speech training, speechreading, reading, and writing.

From the time of the establishment of the first oral schools, oralism as a teaching philosophy has made steady progress. Most oralists demanded the exclusion of any form of manual gesture. The reasons for this rested on the belief that signs would prevent the acquisition of speech skills. Gardiner Hubbard, writing about early attempts to incorporate both articulation training and manualism, indicates the following:

They failed, as they always will fail if attempted in a school where the sign language is the vernacular. A fair trial can only be made where articulation and reading from the lips form the only medium of communication taught, and the only one allowed. The two cannot be carried on together. The language of signs is without doubt more attractive to the deaf-mute, and will be the language of his life if he is encouraged in its use. If the trial is to be made, if experiment is to be fairly and honestly tested, it must be in schools established for that purpose, and under teachers earnestly and heartily engaged in the work, and at least hopeful of success.[7]

Hubbard's statement that sign language would be more attractive to a deaf person is an understatement. Some oralists have recognized that it is in fact a very difficult task to separate a deaf child from the language of signs. Sarah Porter, writing in an article of the *American Annals of the Deaf and Dumb,* noted, "Every oral teacher knows that fighting signs is like fighting original sin. Put deaf children together and they will make signs secretly if not openly in their intercourse with each other."[8]

Many schools were established on the oral philosophy, and most tried to exclude manualism from the premises. Once established, oralism made steady progress. The future looked bright indeed. As Alexander Graham Bell optimistically indicated,

> Where you have a free competition of methods and schools, and a struggle among them for existence, natural selection will surely operate to bring about the survival of the fittest. Time will reveal the best. The indications are very clear that the Oral Method is a growing method in the United States, but only 30 years have elapsed since it was established on American soil.[9]

Between the years 1895 and 1913, the proportion of students taught chiefly by the oral method had more than tripled.[10] Oralism has continued to win adherents during the twentieth century. One staunch supporter was John Dutton Wright, founder of the Wright Oral School. According to Wright (1928),

> Some of the most efficient schools for the deaf in the United States are conducted wholly without either the sign language or finger spelling and their educational results exceed in some cases the best results attained by the "Combined" schools, and in all cases are as good as "Combined" schools of similar type. The use of the sign language and finger spelling is not only unnecessary in educating deaf children, it is really a handicap, and in time will be wholly eliminated from our educational system.[11]

Although history would prove Wright wrong, by the 1930s the promise of oralism had gained widespread acceptance, as indicated by Max Goldstein.

> . . . the deaf no longer destined to be segregated in groups who understand their signs and manual, are now being restored to the larger community, come in contact with their hearing and speaking fellows; qualify to enter higher institutions of learning and take their place with hearing fellow-students in the class and lecture room, and full, useful citizenship in the larger community is theirs.[12]

A yardstick for measuring the educational success of a school program was offered by the *Volta Review* in 1919: "The quality of the school's teaching is good if you can without too much difficulty understand the speech of the totally-deaf-from-birth pupils, and if through lipreading they can understand you."[13]

In terms of education (literacy and knowledge, etc.), understanding speech and intelligible speech as the sole basis for evaluation would seem to be highly inadequate for measuring *educational success.*

ORALISM TODAY

Today, the oral system is usually combined with the auricular (acoustic) method and is often referred to as the aural-oral approach or the auditory-oral approach. Oralism continues to utilize speech, speechreading, reading, and writing, along with auditory training in its educational techniques. The society representing the oral philosophy is the Alexander Graham Bell Association for the Deaf. Central to the oral philosophy is the belief that

> all hearing-impaired children should have the opportunity to learn to speak and understand spoken language. . . that spoken expressive language and academic achievement relative to normal children are the criteria by which the hearing-impaired child is to be judged in society. . . And that the simultaneous teaching of auditory-oral skills and manual skills (are) incompatible with the maximization of auditory-oral communication skills.[14]

A leading authority on oralism states, "If you want your child to talk in a normal way, you must speak to him as you would to any small child, not in an unnatural way. If you persist in using gestures or pantomime he will not trouble to talk."[15] Such an attitude toward manual communication has caused this system to sometimes be labeled *pure oralism.*[16]

Much of the oralist philosophy is rooted in the concept of maximum utilization of residual hearing. *Residual hearing* refers to the "hearing available after damage to the auditory mechanism has already occurred."[17] The idea of maximizing use of this hearing by stimulating the auditory mechanism is not new. A host of devices have been invented since Archigenes advocated the hearing trumpet in the first century.[18]

This concept was espoused in the United States by Gallaudet in the 1880s and particularly emphasized and developed by Max Goldstein in the 1920s, who defined the *acoustic method* as "stimulation or education of the hearing mechanism and its associated sense-organs by sound vibrations as applied either by voice or any sonorous instrument."[19]

A 1976 pamphlet published by the Alexander Graham Bell Association for the Deaf, entitled *Speech and The Use of Residual Hearing,* asks pointedly, "Can meaningful reception ensue with only a small amount of residual hearing?" The pamphlet affirms that the answer is a "resounding 'YES.' ... Armed with up-to-date aural mechanicals, parents and teachers are achieving. Hearing-impaired children are learning to listen and to speak." This unqualified optimism implies that all "hearing-impaired" children can learn to speak. Such extreme optimism is a quality for which the oralists have often been criticized. To be sure, some "educationally" deaf children and most hard-of-hearing children will learn speech (and hopefully language, too) through the utilization of their residual hearing, but most profoundly deaf children (a subgroup of those labeled hearing impaired) will not.

The value of residual hearing for an individual child depends in part upon the force of the sound (decibels or dB) required before the sound can be heard by the child and the frequency range (Hertz or Hz) the child can hear.[20]

It is recognized that most deaf persons have some residual hearing and that many can benefit to a certain extent from amplification. However, the benefits of amplification are dependent upon the pattern and severity of the loss.[21] It must also be remembered that a damaged auditory mechanism transmits distorted or poor-quality impulses that can hinder the brain's ability to interpret the sound signals.[22]

Generally, amplification for the child with a profound hearing loss serves only to create an awareness of sound. "The understanding of distinct sound patterns and speech is impossible. . . [and] there is no evidence to substantiate the notion that sound awareness contributes to the development of a speaking vocabulary or linguistic competence."[23] For the child with a profound hearing loss, amplification "may assist in learning to recognize and respond to environmental sounds — sirens, horns, loud music, and the like — but he cannot hear speech sounds well enough to interpret them or to be significantly influenced in his own speech development."[24]

SPEECHREADING

Another important element of the oralist approach that deserves attention is *speechreading*. This technique was formerly referred to as *lipreading*. Speechreading can be defined as the "art of understanding the speech of others by watching their lips and other facial movements as they talk."[25] Speechreading is an extremely difficult skill for the prelingually deaf child to master, and it has been estimated that only 4 percent of the deaf adults are proficient speechreaders and that a similarly small percentage of prelingually deaf persons develop fully understandable speech.[26]

One difficulty lies in the fact that 40 to 60 percent of English sounds are indistinguishable on the lips.[27] For example, the words *mama, papa,* and *bye-bye* all appear identical when observed on another person's lips. Tests have proven that the best speechreaders are non-deaf persons who are able to use their language base to guess or fill in the words they cannot read. Unfortunately, the prelingually deaf child does not have this language background to use in filling in the gaps, and it is unrealistic to expect him to acquire language skills through the

use of such an inefficient system as speechreading (Fig. 22).[28]
Another drawback to speechreading is the tremendous
amount of attention the child is required to give to the lips.

Figure 22. Speechreading and oral instruction as satirized in *Deaf Spectrum*.
Courtesy of *Deaf Spectrum*, Beaverton, Oregon.

The preschool-age child's play (learning) activities must often be interfered with and disrupted, in order to draw his attention to his mother's mouth, where he will supposedly see a word being formed which is related to his current activity. Such interference understandably may often result in annoyance and anger[29] to the consternation of parents, who are trying to help.

THE COMBINED SYSTEM

Joseph Claybaugh Gordon, an early chronicler and professor at the National College for the Deaf, writing in 1892 indicated that "President Gallaudet recommends a general scheme of instruction, the aim of which is to include 'every method which can be shown to be of real service to any sub-class of the deaf.' This comprehensive scheme is named by President Gallaudet the 'combined system.' "[30]

Actually, the combined system was fairly imprecise, in that it allowed a great deal of teacher leeway. The system that is considered by many to be the forerunner of Total Communication consisted of the components of the oral philosophy plus various elements of manual communication.

After the advent of oralism, many children who failed to progress under oralism were placed in a combined setting. Thus, the combined system became the customary method to use after the oral approach had ended in failure for the child.

Today, there are still schools operating on the same principle. The term *combined system,* as traditionally used, referred to several methods. Because of the flexibility allowed within the classroom, all methods qualified as "combined," as long as any form of manualism was involved. The fact that several methods were utilized under the same rubric has been a longstanding criticism. Joseph Gordon, noting this criticism in 1892, commented, "Dr. E. A. Fay notes not less than ten varieties of methods, differing in matters of detail, all of which are practiced in America under this [combined] designation."[31]

The *American Annals of the Deaf* offered the following definition in its January, 1914, issue of the combined system.

Speech and speech-reading are regarded as very important,

but mental development and the acquisition of language are regarded as still more important. It is believed that in some cases mental development and acquisition of language can be best promoted by the "Manual" or "Manual Alphabet Methods," and, so far as circumstances permit, such method is chosen for each pupil as seems best adapted for his individual case. Speech and speech-reading are taught where the measure of success seems likely to justify the labor expended, and in some of the classrooms and most of the schools some of the pupils are taught wholly or chiefly by the Oral Method or the Auricular Method.[32]

Concerning the above definition, the renowned auralist Max Goldstein commented in 1933, "My impression of this statement is that the 'combined system' is an all-inclusive term and aims to use all of the known methods of teaching the deaf, in the same school. Experience has proven the fallacy of this pedagogy."[33]

We have said that the combined method is still practiced today. Examples of the combined system currently practiced are seen in programs where educational classes are carried out orally, but manual communication is allowed outside the classroom. J. K. Reeves, headmaster of the Whitebrook School in Manchester, England and editor of the *Teacher of the Deaf* magazine describes the procedures employed at his school (1977).

The staff remain united against the use of sign or fingerspelling and the children are positively encouraged to be oral while manualism, which might creep in from outside sources, is discouraged. (It is expected that some older pupils will meet deaf adults outside school and it is expected that signs will be used in communication, but it is additionally understood these must not be used in school because the school is an environment in which speech and lipreading should be practiced at all times.)[34]

Other combined programs allow classes for older children to be conducted as combined classes (that is, utilizing both manual and oral communication), while classes for younger children are exclusively oral.[35]

One form of the combined system is often referred to as the

Rochester Method. This system utilizes simultaneous speech and fingerspelling but excludes the use of sign language. Some schools use the Rochester Method with all the students, while others use it only with older children, restricting the young ones to oral communication. Still others use it with young children, while adding signs at the older levels.

Confusion is apt to arise with the introduction of the word *simultaneous.* Most people use this word interchangeably with the term *combined,* i.e. "the simultaneous method."

The older combined system(s) in their myriad forms may appear at first glance to be a fair alternative to oralism. If a child cannot succeed orally, then he is given a second chance to try manually. In the early years of educating deaf children, it was widely postulated that sign language stood "as a great barrier to the acquisition of language,"[36] and consequently the rationale behind the oral-failure-combined approach may have had some validity in the light of such beliefs. Research, however, has repeatedly revealed the fallacy of such a belief.

Furthermore, several studies have suggested that "there may be 'critical periods' at which different kinds of behavior are most effectively learned and incorporated. If such learning does not take place at the appropriate times, it may be less completely learned and may break down in times of stress."[37] It is widely hypothesized that language has a biological timetable: "an interlocking motoric and linguistic developmental schedule."[38] It is believed that the ages from two to six are the critical years for symbolization and conceptualization. "We accelerate in those years in the rate of our capacity to learn language and may thereafter reach a plateau or even decline in this most vital of all human abilities."[39] With this in mind, the question then becomes: Can we really afford to gamble these precious early years on the chance that a child may learn to speak when the stakes are so high? Is speech worth so much that we are willing to risk sacrificing language for it? Apparently, for the oralist, it is.

> Reducing or abandoning our best efforts to teach speech to deaf persons is to deny them the opportunity for an achievement unique to man — the development of an acoustic code

that enables a human being to communicate with his fellow human being in a distinctive way that is not possible through any other mode of communication . . .

. . . oral success depends upon the practice of oral communication skills both in and outside the classroom.

Language is the tool of communication and must be used expressively to convey thoughts and emotions and to give information to family, neighbors, friends, suppliers of services, merchants, and the general public.[40]

For some oralists, success depends on more than communicative ability. Reeves observes that for graduates of the Whitebrook School, "Those aspects that were important seemed to be a good oral attitude with the expectancy to have to cope in a speaking environment, a pleasant and stable personality with a willingness to adapt to circumstances as required, and *above all, an eagerness to please and be pleasant* [emphasis ours]."[41] Reeves has called his system of education *The Whole Personality Approach to Oralism.*

IS TOTAL COMMUNICATION THE SAME AS THE COMBINED SYSTEM?

It has often been postulated that the system advocated within the framework of Total Communication is nothing more than the older combined system. This, of course, is a matter for interpretation. We have said that for the most part the combined system usually began with two strikes against it — that is, with an oral failure and after critical learning periods had passed. A Total Communication approach starts at the beginning, even before the child is emerging from his infancy.

More important, Total Communication is not a system, but a philosophy that incorporates the combined system *and* the oral system and whatever else is necessary to put the child at the center of our attention. In some instances, it might not be appropriate to utilize such procedures as sign language; in many cases it would be appropriate. The main objective is that the system revolves around the child to best utilize his learning potential.

In making a comparison between the Total Communication philosophy and the combined system, one cannot but note an inherent difference with respect to attitudes involved — and in particular to the way we view the child, who is the end-result of the educational process.

The pupil with a background in the combined approach and communicating manually was usually regarded as an educational failure. Sign language has traditionally been the stigma of deafness and a mark of shame, and the student bore that mark. Proponents of Total Communication view sign language as a legitimate language and as a thing of beauty; not something that "creeps in" once the teacher's back is turned. Educators who adhere to the Total Communication philosophy try to impart to the students a sense of pride in their educational accomplishments, as well as in themselves as potential leaders of the deaf community. This fundamental difference in attitude is conveyed to the deaf youngster and is likewise at the heart of the Deaf Pride movement.

Total Communication is a natural consequence of a system

Figure 23. The rise of Total Communication, shown in *Deaf Spectrum*. Courtesy of *Deaf Spectrum*, Beaverton, Oregon.

hampered by inadequacies — the combined method. While it may incorporate much, Total Communication should not be viewed as being the same as the combined method with a new name. Total Communication allows us to utilize any and all communicative systems or modes as may be necessary to remove those inadequacies. Total Communication could be the keystone which will enable us to rewrite the old equation of

the oral failure + the combined method = educational failure

to a new equation of

Total Communication = better communication + increased resources = educational success!

REFERENCES

1. Richard G. Brill, "Total Communication as A Basis of Educating Prelingually Deaf Children." In *Communication Symposium* (Frederick, Maryland: Maryland Schools for the Deaf, 1970), p. 10.
2. Joseph Claybaugh Gordon, *Notes and Observations Upon the Education of the Deaf* (Washington, D.C.: Volta Bureau, 1892), p. xlvii.
3. *Ibid.*, p. xlix.
4. Mabel Gardiner Bell, "Introduction." In Gardiner G. Hubbard, *The Story of the Rise of the Oral Method in America, as Told in the Writing of the Late Hon. Gardiner G. Hubbard* (Washington, D.C.: Press of W. F. Roberts, 1898), p. 9.
5. *Ibid.*
6. "Methods of Instruction in American Schools for the Deaf," *American Annals of the Deaf*, Jan. 1914, p. 41.
7. Gardiner G. Hubbard, *The Story of the Rise of the Oral Method in America as Told in the Writings of the Hon. Gardiner G. Hubbard* (Washington, D.C.: Press of W. F. Roberts, 1898), p. 20.
8. Harry Best, *The Deaf* (New York: Thomas Y. Crowell Company, 1914), p. 284.
9. John Dutton Wright, *The Little Deaf Child* (New York: Wright Oral School, 1928), p. 154.
10. Max A. Goldstein, *Problems of the Deaf* (St. Louis: Laryngoscope Press, 1933), p. 41.
11. "Choosing a School for the Deaf," *Volta Review*, 51, 12:596, 1949.
12. "A Position Paper of the American Organization for the Education of the Hearing Impaired, May 1, 1975," *Volta Review*, 77, 5:330-334, 1975.
13. *Volta Review*, 51, 12:596, 1949.
14. "A Position Paper of the American Organization for the Hearing Impaired, May 1, 1975," *Volta Review*, 77, 5:330-332, 1975.
15. William H. Cooksley, Jr., "Communication in the Education of the Deaf:

A Position Paper," *Deaf Spectrum, 4,* 7:10, 1973.

16. Samuel A. Kirk, *Educating Exceptional Children,* 2nd ed. (Boston: Houghton Mifflin Company, 1972), pp. 265-266.

17. Eugene D. Mindel and McCay Vernon, *They Grow in Silence; The Deaf Child and His Family* (Silver Spring, Maryland: National Association of the Deaf, 1971), p. 34.

18. Goldstein, p. 207.

19. *Ibid,* p. 215.

20. Mindel and Vernon, pp. 34-35.

21. Hilde S. Schlesinger and Kathryn P. Meadow, *Sound and Sign: Childhood Deafness and Mental Health* (Berkeley: University of California Press, 1972), pp. 1-2.

22. Mindel and Vernon, p. 31.

23. *Ibid.,* p. 34.

24. Lee Katz, Steve L. Mathis III, and Edward C. Merrill, Jr., *The Deaf Child in the Public Schools; A Handbook for Parents of Deaf Children* (Danville, Illinois: Interstate Printers and Publishers, 1974), p. 6.

25. Marjorie E. Magner, "Parents Can Help Deaf Children to Acquire Ability in Speechreading." In Powire Vaux Doctor (ed.), *Communication with the Deaf* (Washington, D.C.: American Annals of the Deaf, 1969), p. 21.

26. Schlesinger and Meadow, p. 50.

27. Mindel and Vernon, p. 96.

28. Brill, p. 11.

29. Mindel and Vernon, p. 58.

30. Gordon, p. viii.

31. *Ibid.,* p. ix.

32. "Methods of Instruction in American Schools for the Deaf," p. 41.

33. Goldstein, p. 206.

34. J. K. Reeves, "Scope for Oralism," *Volta Review, 79, 1:*52, 1977.

35. Brill, p. 10.

36. Harry Best, *The Deaf* (New York: Thomas Y. Crowell Company, 1914), p. 279.

37. Schlesinger and Meadow, p. 12.

38 *Ibid.,* p. 56.

39. Boyce R. Williams, "Some Thoughts on Total Communication." In *Communication Symposium* (Frederick, Maryland: Maryland School for the Deaf, 1970), p. 15.

40. Helen S. Lane, "Thoughts on Oral Advocacy Today . . . With Memories of the Society of Oral Advocates," *Volta Review, 78, 3:*138, 1976.

41. Reeves, p. 48.

CHAPTER 4

TOTAL COMMUNICATION

STIRRINGS OF DISCONTENT

BY the 1950s, oralism was firmly established as the accepted and dominant method for educating deaf children in the United States. The oral system was usually used in conjunction with the acoustic system. An alternative to the oral system was the combined system — a system which allowed the use of manual communication either full- or part-time, depending on circumstances and which was usually employed after a child had failed to advance in a purely "oral" environment. For the most part, it was a system restricted in practice to state-supported residential schools.

The Rochester Method — simultaneous use of fingerspelling and speech — had been in existence since 1878 when first originated by Zenas Freeman Westervelt at the Rochester School for the Deaf. This system remained in use until the mid-1940s and then gradually decreased in popularity. However, according to Leonard M. Elstad, even though the Rochester Method was still used in some instances, by 1955, "There [were] no schools for the deaf . . . that [did] not start all children orally in the classroom."[1]

Yet in the 1950s, stirrings of discontent within the profession became apparent. There emerged a sizable segment of professionals in the fields of education, psychology, and deafness who declared the need to develop a "philosophical framework" which would recognize the psychological implications of deafness as it affects individuals and deal with those implications in an intelligent and rational manner. It was felt that ability rather than weakness should be emphasized, and the value of manual communication as a useful addition to the aural-oral approach was advocated, despite pressures from the advocates of oralism.[2] Once again, the battle was on.

THE ORIGINS OF TOTAL COMMUNICATION

The term *Total Communication* as applied to the deaf made its appearance in the late 1960s. Roy K. Holcomb, a deaf educator and parent of two deaf children, was first to use the term. When he became area supervisor of the Santa Ana, California, program for the hearing impaired, he was instrumental in establishing Total Communication as the philosophy of the school.[3] However, it was not until 1976 that an official definition of Total Communication was adopted at a meeting of the Conference of Executives of American Schools for the Deaf (CEASD) in Rochester, New York, in May, 1976. A committee had been appointed for the express purpose of arriving at a definition of *Total Communication* acceptable to the Conference of Executives. As a result of this committee report, Total Communication is now defined by CEASD as "a philosophy incorporating the appropriate aural, manual, and oral modes of communication in order to ensure effective communication with and among hearing-impaired persons."[4]

Although there are still many varying opinions concerning Total Communication as an appropriate educational philosophy for deaf children, gains in its acceptance during the past decade have been tremendous. Data collected by I. K. Jordan, Gerilee Gustason, and Roslyn Rosen reveal that, during the 1975-1976 school year, the overwhelming trend with respect to deaf children was toward Total Communication.* These researchers conducted a national survey of 796 programs for the hearing impaired and noted that, of the 343 programs that had reported a change in communication mode within the classroom, 333 (97%) had changed *to* Total Communication.[5]† The number of classes reported in the survey using various communication modes were as follows:

---

*For the purposes of the survey research, Total Communication was defined as a "method of communication" utilized within the classroom.

†Of those programs reporting change, "5 changed to the Oral/Aural method and 8 changed from Total Communication. . ."[5]

Total Communication	4,619
Oral-Aural	2,370
Rochester Method	155
Cued Speech	37

Thus, according to the responses the researchers received, Total Communication was the method used in 65 percent of classes in programs responding to the survey (*see* Appendix A).

TOTAL COMMUNICATION ENDORSED BY DEAF PERSONS THEMSELVES

The Total Communication concept is presently the educational philosophy officially endorsed by the National Association of the Deaf (NAD), which boasts a membership in excess of 15,000, and the National Fraternal Society of the Deaf (FRAT), with a membership exceeding 13,000. That is to say, Total Communication is endorsed by deaf persons themselves — a fact not to be taken lightly.[6]

A CHILD-CENTERED PHILOSOPHY

Naturally, many factors have contributed to the widespread acceptance of Total Communication. Although it would be difficult to identify all the related influences, some of the more obvious ones are worthy of consideration.

Most noticeably, the success of Total Communication involves the educators' (and other professionals') concern

TOTAL COMMUNICATION
TO BETTER EDUCATE THE DEAF CHILD

SPONSORED BY

NEW JERSEY ASSOCIATION OF THE DEAF, INC.

Figure 24. A bumper sticker developed by the New Jersey Association of the Deaf indicating grass roots support for Total Communication. Courtesy of the New Jersey Association for the Deaf.

for the welfare of the deaf child. Without the help and support of various professionals, the concept of Total Communication probably would not have survived. The concern springs largely from limitations of the traditional methods of educating deaf children. These shortcomings are best reflected in the poor educational achievement levels of most deaf students (Appendix B).

ACHIEVEMENT LEVELS

In the 1960s several studies were conducted to investigate the

Figure 25. "Whose Responsibility?" (for educational failure). Professionals going in circles. As portrayed in *Deaf Spectrum*. Courtesy of *Deaf Spectrum*, Beaverton, Oregon.

academic achievement and progress of deaf students — and the
results were quite disconcerting. In 1962, one such study by
Schein and Bushnaq reported that only 1.7 percent of the deaf
school-age population attended college.[7] In 1965 and 1966, in-
dependent studies by Boatner and McClure revealed the following:

1. Thirty percent of the students were functionally illiterate.
2. Sixty percent were at grade level 5.3 or below.
3. Only 5 percent achieved tenth-grade level or better — and
   most of these students were hard of hearing or had become
   deaf later in life.[8]

The results of these studies are particularly depressing, since
the IQ level for the deaf population is comparable to that of the
hearing population.[9]

Raymond J. Trybus and Michael A. Karchner from the Office of Demographic Studies at Gallaudet College have reported
the results of the National Achievement Test Standardization
Program conducted by their office in 1974.[10] Their report indicates that half of the twenty-year-old deaf student population
reads below the mid-fourth-grade level and that only 10 percent
of hearing-impaired eighteen-year-olds can read above the
eighth-grade level. With respect to math computations, 10 percent of hearing-impaired chidren reach the level of difficulty
attained by the average hearing child of the same age, with the
great majority still well below their hearing counterparts (*see*
Appendix B.).

ON AN EMOTIONAL PLANE

Other factors contributing to the acceptance of the Total
Communication philosophy can be found on a more emotional
level. The increasing number of "sad stories" that have circu-
lated among professionals in the field have caused many persons to step back and reevaluate their teaching priorities. A
good example is illustrated by a story which appeared in the
August 1969 issue of the *New Republic* magazine. In an article

by James Ridgeway entitled "Dumb Children," the failure of an educational approach that was not child centered was related. "Not long ago I spoke with the lady director of an oral school. She was telling about her program, disparaging signs as 'glorified gestures.' Finally she pointed to a little black girl, hearing aids sprouting from both ears, who was sitting on the floor and staring at us: 'Look at her; she's such a well-trained animal!' "[11]

Although the above is an extreme example, it does illustrate what can happen when speech is regarded as the criterion for humanness. Such statements convey the idea that without speech one cannot truly be a human being. A familiar advertisement appearing regularly in the *Volta Review* reads:

> The news that our 15-month-old son, Larry, was profoundly deaf came as a numbing shock. The diagnosis left one thought: Will Larry learn to live in the hearing world or will he live in silence, a mute, a burden to his family and society?
>
> Six years later found Larry in a regular first grade class . . . a happy, confident, chattering child with excellent speech. Larry had been rescued from the fate of silence and brought into the world of sound.[12]

Implicit in this statement is that deafness, per se, means being a burden to family and society, while speech is nothing short of a panacea for all of life's problems.

A SIGN OF THE TIMES

Less obvious factors contributing to the acceptance of Total Communication as a philosophy are found by examining the decade from which the concept emerged. Most people will recall the 1960s as being characterized by turmoil and social reform. One positive outcome of this strife was a heightened sensitivity to minority groups and the value of their distinct characteristics.[13] On one hand, society became more aware of these people and their respective rights; conversely, minorities began asserting themselves and taking pride in their own unique qualities. Deaf persons as one such group were no exception. It is not surprising that the trend of self-awareness and acceptance was reflected in the deaf population, as well as that of other groups. Along with the American Indians' growing appreciation of their heritage and the pronouncement that "Black is Beautiful," there was also a Deaf Pride movement (Figs. 26 and 27).

OUT FROM SOCIETY'S DEGRADATION

An interesting analogy can be drawn when a comparison of some of the things blacks were subjected to in their unique history is made with some of the educational practices found in schools for deaf children. In the *Autobiography of Malcolm X,* the author describes the method by which blacks attempted to straighten their hair in order to have the same texture as that of whites. In Malcolm X's youth, this was an accepted custom, though exceedingly painful and potentially dangerous. The process, *conking,* consisted of applying treatments of a formula containing lye, among other ingredients, to one's scalp.

Figure 26. Deaf Pride symbol, as illustrated in *Deaf Spectrum.* Courtesy of *Deaf Spectrum,* Beaverton, Oregon.

Figure 27. Deaf Awareness symbol. Deaf Awareness Year One was sponsored by the Registry of Interpreters for the Deaf. Courtesy of Mary Jane Rhodes, Greenbelt, Maryland.

Straight hair — like that of Caucasians — was the accepted standard of attractiveness. To achieve this desired outcome, one would subject himself to the most unbearable discomfort.

> A jelly-like, starchy-looking glop resulted from the lye and potatoes, and Shorty broke in the two eggs, stirring real fast — his own conk and dark face bent down close. The congolene turned pale-yellowish. "Feel the jar," Shorty said. I cupped my hand against the outside, and snatched it away. "Damn right, it's hot, that's the lye," he said. "So you know it's going to burn when I comb it in — it burns bad. But the longer you can stand it, the straighter the hair." . . . Then from the big Vaseline® jar, he took a handful and massaged it hard all through my hair and into the scalp . . .
>
> I gritted my teeth and tried to pull the sides of the kitchen table together. The comb felt as if it was raking my skin off. My eyes watered, my nose was running. I couldn't stand it any longer; I bolted to the washbasin.

Later, upon reflection of this practice, Malcolm X concludes:

> How ridiculous I was! Stupid enough to stand there simply lost in admiration of my hair now looking "white" reflected

in the mirror in Shorty's room. I vowed that I'd never again
be without a conk, and I never was for many years.

This was my first really big step toward self-degradation:
when I endured all of that pain, literally burning my flesh to
have it look like a white man's hair.[15]

What, you might ask, does this story have to do with the deaf
population of our society? For one thing, it is an extreme example of what can happen when a group of people must accept
the standards of those who are outside their group. If we compare this tragic procedure so many blacks underwent with some
practices deaf children have been subjected to, it is not difficult
to see similarities.

Just as kinky hair was thought to be unattractive by white
society, so manual communication was thought to be inappropriate by the "hearing world." Malcolm X tried to deny his
blackness by conking his hair and, in doing so, was guilty of
self-degradation. Similarly, many parents of deaf children and
some educational institutions try to deny the children's deafness by forcing them to adhere to a method of education that
deprives the children of their greatest learning asset, vision, and
a way to utilize that asset: communication via a visual system.*
Relying on a visually based means of communication has the
potential for communication far superior to speechreading,
which relies on the visual channel for understanding an aurally
based system.

But manual communication has long been considered a
stigma of deafness by society. Parents who feel stigmatized in-
sist that their children be schooled in a manner which, for all
practical purposes, denies their deafness and tries to make them
resemble a hearing child as nearly as possible. Such a youngster
grows up with serious unresolved questions concerning his
own worth as a human being. As noted by Hilde S. Schlesinger
and Kathryn P. Meadow in their book *Sound and Sign*, "As in
the case of blacks, or immigrants, the most successful identifi-
cations may occur in those individuals who accept the differences imposed by color, language, or minority group mores.

---

*Speechreading, too, relies on vision. However, its ambiguity precludes its effectiveness
as a learning-communicative channel for the majority of deaf students.

The successful individual may thus live in many worlds; the alienated individual may be a stranger in all."[16]

An extreme example of self-denial occurs when a deaf person attempts to deny his own deafness. One such incident is related by Eugene Mindel and McCay Vernon in the book *They Grow in Silence*.

> One of the authors (E.D.M.) once asked a profoundly deaf ten-year-old boy if he knew sign language, whereupon the boy answered, "No, that's for deaf-mutes." It is as if he regarded himself as a hearing person "temporarily out of order," who with the proper concentration on speech and speechreading would become like everyone else, like his parents' and teachers' fantasies would have him become. Thus, the children and the parents share a delusional system with eventual "recovery" from deafness at its core. Deaf children, their parents, relatives and friends, and the child's teachers all participate in the perpetration of this tragic delusion.[7]

But why does the contempt for manual communication exist? Oralists have fought for years against acceptance of sign language and implied, when not stating outright, that it is an inferior mode of communication. In 1966, the chief executive of the Alexander Graham Bell Association, George Fellendorf, sent the following telegram to the president of NBC protesting the display of sign language on television:

> We would like to discuss with your representative at the earliest possible date your announced plans for a documentary on the deaf scheduled for "NBC Experiment in Television." Continuing to display sign language on nationwide TV destroys the efforts of thousands of parents of deaf children and teachers of the deaf who are trying to teach deaf children to speak. This program will evoke unfavorable reaction from educators and parents and the informed public. We assume you are interested in this audience.[18]

In another incident involving the presentation of the National Theater of the Deaf on television, Fellendorf sent a memorandum to his board of directors calling for a letter-writing campaign "so that we can effectively counteract this effort to make sign language of the deaf to be an artistic form to be encouraged in the theater, televised in the homes of parents and employees, and quite likely emulated in educational and parental circles."[19]

The development of sign language as a stigma is not easy to trace. Some feel it might have emerged in the early part of the history of our country when "talking with hands" was characteristic of the new immigrant and lower economic classes.[20] Mindel and Vernon suggest that "gestural communication is so intertwined with early infantile experience 'left behind' in the unconscious that for some to consider its use threatens them with eruption of primitive thoughts and impulses they have long struggled to keep in check."[21]

Schlesinger and Meadow point out that traditionally society has not been kind to its exceptional members. Those who are different have often been excluded from and/or denied society's benefits. Sign language emphasizes differences and "deafness more than other disabilities appears to frighten the uninitiated into a 'shock-withdrawal-paralysis' reaction on their first exposure."[22]

But whatever the reasons, the stigma is dying, and we can see quite a reverse trend today. Manual communication is literally permeating the hearing man's culture. Society is not only accepting manual communication — it is enjoying it. For this, much credit must go to the captivating performances of the National Theater of the Deaf.[23]

Television, despite the opposition from diehard oralists, has played a role in the growing popularity of sign language. Adults and children have been exposed to sign language and fingerspelling in a host of shows, including *Sesame Street, Police Woman, 60 Minutes,* and others. There has also been an increase in manual communication publications, and the children's book *Handtalk,* by Remy Charlip, won Honorable Mention Junior in the Children's Science Book Awards sponsored by the New York Academy of Science.

There are classes throughout the country for learning manual communication skills at the high school and college levels. Some schools have accepted proficiency in this communication mode as the equivalent of a second language. Increased interest in sign language is also reflected in organizations whose function is to serve the deaf community. For over a decade, the National Registry of Interpreters for the Deaf has been endeavoring to develop certification of interpreters. The National Association of the Deaf has added a new component to its organization, SIGN (Sign Instructor's Guidance Network). Another program which has been seeking to develop more skilled interpreters is the National Interpreter Training Consortium.[24]

Finally, it must be noted that the increased independence and sensibility of the deaf population has aided the acceptance of sign language. There are an increasing number of deaf persons at management levels of education, government, and industry.[25] The most recent example is the naming of a deaf person to the superintendency of the Louisiana School for the Deaf — the first such appointment of a state residential school chief administrative officer in the United States in the twentieth century. Deaf people are a group to be recognized, and they are seeking a voice in the forces which affect their lives — one of these being education. This awareness is reflected in the resolution endorsing Total Communication by the members of the largest fraternal organization for deaf persons, the FRAT: "Whereas the ultimate consumers of communication methodology for the hearing impaired *are the hearing impaired themselves* [emphasis ours]."

Deaf citizens have united to proclaim they will no longer sit idly by and let the "others" (no matter how well intentioned) tell them what is best for them — which standards to accept as their own. They have learned there are more important things than "an eagerness to please and be pleasant." The membership of the National Association of the Deaf and other organizations have come together and are letting their influence be felt.

SIGN LANGUAGE AND TOTAL COMMUNICATION

Sign language is the hallmark of the deaf community.[27] Many believe that sign language "fulfills the requirements of a genuine language."[28] Yet, as we have noted, sign language has for a long time been disparaged by society. Only in recent years has there been a significant change in attitudes towards the sign language of the deaf. This change in attitude is embodied in the Total Communication movement.

Sign language is still not approved by the so-called pure oralist. The various combined systems generally use specific methods of manual communication (often with restricted groups of children or when the teacher's back is turned) on an incomplete basis.

Total Communication, however, dictates the use of all the elements of instruction utilized by the oralists and accepts all forms of manual communication as equally valid tools. It should be noted here that there is no exclusively manual system for educating deaf children. Although many educators do promote the use of manual communication, they also recognize the value of amplification and the development of speech and speechreading skills, to the extent that these abilities are possible for the individual child. Obviously, proponents of Total Communication do not wish to deprive deaf children of speech; but neither do they want to deprive them of language acquisition and mental development — goals taking precedence over speech. As Dr. McCay Vernon noted in an article aptly entitled "Mind Over Mouth," research has shown that the use of manual communication actually enhances greater achievement levels in deaf children. This includes such skills as written language and reading skills, and it also facilitates language development.[29] Furthermore, it has been noted that deaf children of deaf parents have been found to have a distinct advantage in many areas of cognitive and psychological functions, compared to deaf children of hearing parents. Hilde Schlesinger and Kathryn Meadow hypothesize this is so because of "the early possibility of parent-child communication by means of manual language."[30]

Despite research findings, traditionalists continue to demand that manual communication be excluded from the classroom. Yet, sign language is unequivocally one of the most "useful coping mechanisms of deafness."[31] Because it is so important for so many reasons, it is an integral component of Total Communication. This relatively new philosophy can be said to encompass the change in society's attitude toward sign language and toward deaf persons themselves. Deaf persons today are not maligned for communicating manually. They are not forced by society to feel shame or self-degradation because they have not acquired the skills of speech considered "acceptable" by others. It is not their imperfections that are stressed, but their achievements and abilities. The deaf community is and should be viewed as a valuable segment of society whose potential must not be wasted. Aside from considering only what we can offer deaf persons, now there is concern for what they can offer us — and each other.

REFERENCES

1. Leonard M. Elstad, "The Deaf," In M. E. Frampton and E. D. Gall (eds.), *Special Education for the Exceptional* (Boston: Porter Sargent Publisher, 1955), vol. 2, p. 159.
2. Mervin D. Garretson, "Total Communication," *Volta Review*, 78, 4:89, 1966.
3. *Ibid.*
4. *Defining Total Communication* (Rochester, New York: Conference of Executives of American Schools for the Deaf, A Committee Report, 1976), p. 3.
5. I. K. Jordan, Gerilee Gustason, and Roslyn Rosen, "Current Communication Trends at Programs for the Deaf," *American Annals of the Deaf, 121,* 6:531, 1976.
6. McCay Vernon, "Mind Over Mouth: A Rationale for 'Total Communication,'" *Volta Review, 74,* 9:530, 1972.
7. Eugene D. Mindel and McCay Vernon, *They Grow in Silence; The Deaf Child and His Family* (Silver Spring, Maryland: National Association of the Deaf, 1971), p. 91.
8. *Ibid.*
9. *Ibid.,* p. 87.
10. Raymond J. Trybus and Michael A. Karchmer, "School Achievement Scores of Hearing Impaired Children: National Data on Achievement Status and Growth Patterns," *American Annals of the Deaf, 122,* 2:62-69, 1977.
11. James Ridgeway, "Dumb Children," *New Republic, 161,* 5:21, 1969.
12. Advertisement from the Larry Jarret Memorial Foundation, printed on a regular basis in *Volta Review.*

13. Garretson, p. 95.
14. Malcolm X, *The Autobiography of Malcolm X* (New York: Grove Press, 1965), p. 53.
15. *Ibid.,* p. 54.
16. Hilde S. Schlesinger and Kathryn P. Meadow, *Sound and Sign; Childhood Deafness and Mental Health* (Berkeley: University of California Press, 1972), p. 23.
17. Mindel and Vernon, p. 86.
18. Ridgeway, p. 20.
19. *Ibid.,* p. 21.
20. Mindel and Vernon, p. 63.
21. *Ibid.,* p. 84.
22. Schlesinger and Meadow, p. 19.
23. Garretson, p. 95.
24. "The Editor's Page," *Deaf American, 29,* 5:2, 1977.
25. Garretson, p. 95.
26. Resolution of the 1971 Convention of National Fraternal Society of the Deaf, held in Chicago, Illinois adopting Total Communication.
27. Schlesinger and Meadow, p. 3.
28. *Ibid.,* p. 50.
29. Vernon, p. 529.
30. Schlesinger and Meadow, p. 51.
31. *Ibid.,* p. 19.

CHAPTER 5

CONSIDERATIONS IN IMPLEMENTING TOTAL COMMUNICATION

Glenn T. Lloyd, Ed.D.

ACCOUNTABILITY IN EDUCATION

ACCOUNTABILITY is a serious issue in education today, resulting at least in part from the public's general dissatisfaction with educational results, or achievement on the part of students. The news media has helped in focusing attention on the fact that the costs of education to the taxpayer have soared while the quality of education has, at best, failed to improve. Cases have been reported of graduates from public high schools who are barely able to read and write bringing suit against school districts for their failures. Such suits are based on the premise that the schools are obligated to, in fact, educate the student, and the student's failure is the school district's responsibility.

Taxpayers are becoming increasingly reluctant to pay the educational bill without evidence that the results justify the costs. Such evidence is what accountability is all about.[1] Simply stated, accountability is the "accounting of costs as they relate to the product produced. In education this product is the learned student."[2] Accountability involves the "acceptance of personal responsibility for the achievement of predetermined measurable objectives."[3]

In education, the concept of accountability is directly related to the establishment of goals and objectives. Goals, generally, tend to be stated in terms of long-range global results which may require one or several years to achieve. Too, they tend not to be easily measurable and are oftentimes reflections of societal values. Objectives, by contrast, are statements of behaviors; clear statements of what the learner will do, the conditions under which he will do, and how well he will do. Objectives are ordinarily arranged sequentially (developmentally) and lead to the point at which it is reasonable to state that the learner has accomplished a particular goal. Utilization of this approach helps the teacher in determining a child's accomplishments and needs every step of the way through the educational process. It provides a means of feedback and evaluation that serves education in much the same way that loran serves modern ships.[4]

ACCOUNTABILITY IN PROGRAMS
FOR DEAF CHILDREN

On the basis of the preceding discussion, familiarity with the results of educational programs for deaf children leads to the conclusion that accountability has not been a major concern of education in the past.[5] Data gathered and reported by various researchers reveals some rather disturbing facts. For example, it has been reported that over half of the adult deaf population has not completed high school and that 28 percent of those who have been graduated have finished with no better than an eighth-grade level of achievement.[6] Data from the Office of Demographic Studies at Gallaudet College reveals that the average deaf student is consistently several years behind his hearing peers at all school levels. It is erroneous to conclude that because a deaf student has been graduated from a school for the deaf he has attained an educational level equal to that of his hearing peers. In fact, studies of the reading level of deaf graduates reveal that their average reading level is rarely beyond the third- to fifth-grade level. It seems the success of our educational program in accomplishing the goal of educated graduates has been minimal at best. That it is a necessary consequence of deafness to be relatively uneducated in spite of twelve or more years in an educational program is simply an intolerable assumption.

TOTAL COMMUNICATION AND ACHIEVEMENT LEVELS

It has been variously contended that the primary reason deaf graduates tend to be so poorly educated is that effective communication has been lacking, especially during the earlier, formative years. All too often, the claim is made that, in effect, Total Communication will resolve the problem. Such a position is far too simplistic and untrue. What may be more accurate is the position that educational achievement is largely dependent upon effective interpersonal communication and mastery of English and that the most likely means of achieving that mastery of English, for deaf children, is through using Total Communication.

To reiterate, Total Communication is not, nor can it become, a panacea for the resolution of the educational problems of deaf children. It does seem to offer a practical means by which the doors of educational opportunity may be opened wide enough so that the majority of deaf children may achieve educational parity with their hearing peers. However, the degree of success it will engender is in the hands, literally, of those involved with its implementation. In addition, accountability can become an ally instead of the threat it is so often assumed to be.

COMMUNICATION CRITICISMS AND PROBLEMS

The predominant trend in communication practices in education programs for deaf children is toward Total Communication and away from a strictly oral-aural approach.[7] Despite the trend, many critics of Total Communication state their views, very often, in terms of problems which may occur. In most cases, the stated problems are presented as deleterious effects on children. That there are potential trouble spots should not be denied. Rather, they should be identified and dealt with in order to diminish or eliminate them to the benefit of the child. To that end, let us consider some of those criticisms.

Criticism I — We cannot expect the rest of the world (more than 99%) to learn to sign just to accommodate deaf people.

Who could or would argue with the above statement? Our

own reaction is a "so-what" response. It has never been stated that a goal of teaching everyone to sign is necessary. On the contrary, it is recognized that, while it would be nice if it happened, the fact is that it will not happen, and therefore, every effort must be made to assist each deaf child to develop his oral communication skills in addition to becoming educated. Proponents of Total Communication believe the first priority in the education of deaf children is education. The fact is that the educational achievement levels of deaf graduates from programs for deaf students have been abominable.[8] The major reason for our failures is that the prerequisite to education appears to have been lacking. That is, unless one becomes proficient in the *language* of education, in this case, English, real achievement simply cannot occur. Thus, as Total Communication is implemented and children are, in fact, afforded the opportunity to develop mastery of English, real education becomes possible.

Now, it is not true to say that Total Communication can be a panacea for all our education ills; far from it. If it were true that mastery of English could guarantee real education, we would not be graduating so many normally hearing illiterates with, however, at least average capabilities from our regular high school programs. Yet, unless there is the ability to communicate in the appropriate language, we really cannot be expected to accomplish much higher than a level of functional illiteracy on the part of deaf students in our programs.

Yet Sign Language is Catching On —
An Interesting Example

Morganton, North Carolina, is in a county with only two high schools. Both of those high schools offer an elective to students in manual communication. The first year (1973) it was offered in only one of the two high schools. The second year (1974) both high schools offered it. For those first two years, volunteer teachers taught. Commencing in 1975, the county authorized and hired a regular faculty member to teach the course, which fulfills a speech or drama requirement or which may be taken as an elective. Each quarter, three times each year, a total of five classes are taught between the two high schools; an overall total of fifteen classes. The course is so popular it is limited to seniors, and every section has consistently had a full enrollment and occasionally an overload.[6] We may not be able to teach the world to sign, but in Burke County, North Carolina, at least 375 high school students per year learn manual communication skills. The same is happening in other school systems in North Carolina and in other states too. Do you realize the consequences if ninety-nine more high school programs had the same results every year? It would seem that a few candles have been lit.

Criticism II — Signing is easy and speech is difficult: Given a choice, as the child has under Total Communication, he will choose sign and may never learn to speak.

There are really two parts to this point. As far as the child choosing the easier way, can we help but wonder at the spuriousness of this point? Think about it. How often, when confronted with a choice, one of which looks easier, how often do *you* choose the more difficult way — deliberately? Granted, there are masochistic types who might. Most people seem to prefer the easiest, most comfortable method of achieving what they want. In our judgment, this is not atypical. For the deaf child, if primary reliance by him is on the manual forms of his language and he is able to conquer that language in a comparatively briefer period of time, why not? It might even be that his ego development, his overall mental health could be enhanced because of a facility to express himself and to be understood; to understand when someone speaks to or around him.

Criticism III — In a Total Communication program won't the child's speech suffer?

It is possible the child's speech will suffer; it is always possible that we have to give up something in order to gain something. It is oftentimes a decision we must make based on our value systems: "Which of two possibilities is of greater moment for me?" It is doubtful that the deaf child is confronted with this decision at the conscious level. Regardless, and we do not want to stray too far, not a single study concerned with the effects of Total Communication on the speech development of deaf children supports the contention that the speech will suffer. The few existing studies may report an initial decrease in amount of speech activity, but after a relatively brief time, the speech of children in Total Communication programs has consistently been adjudged to be equal to the speech of children in oral programs.[9,14] Also consistently, results from the studies indicate that the Total Communication children tend to have better speechreading skills. This is an impressive result. It is doubtful that a sufficient number of definitive studies have been accomplished as yet, but if the studies which have been done are any indication, more is accomplished through Total Communication programs.

Yet, one cannot help but wonder whether a real concern is not appropriate, with respect to speech development. It would certainly appear that there must be a basis for concern when we see articles appearing emphasizing the importance of speech in a Total Communication program.[14] Herein may be an illustration of the third criticism of Total Communication; that speech development does tend to get overlooked. Without a sincere, concerted, coordinated, continuing program of speech development, improvement, and correction, it does stand to reason that speech will be slighted to the real, potential disadvantage of the child. Since teachers operating in a Total Communication program apparently feel the need to reemphasize speech work, it would certainly appear that the danger exists of losing a suitable emphasis on oral skills for deaf children.

POTENTIAL PROBLEMS

Attitudes

One of the prime areas of potential problems is that of attitudes — attitudes of teachers and/or supervisors. Recognizing that almost 35 percent of all classes of deaf children are still oral-aural[15] and that the trend is toward Total Communication, attitudinal factors can become crucial. For example, several years ago the chief administrator of a school for deaf children announced on virtually the last day of the school year that, beginning in September, the school would require that all teachers incorporate manual communication into their instructional procedures. We do not have to wonder about attitudes there, even amongst faculty who very much supported the idea. It was not the change that bothered the teachers, it was simply the high-handed way in which it was announced. The school established policy by fiat, but the implementation was far from effective.

In a sense, when a new policy, such as Total Communication, is established or attempted to be established, it is not a strictly administrative prerogative. Such a policy may, in a very real sense, conflict with value systems of individual teachers to such a degree that, practically speaking, nothing changes. Programs and program administrators must reckon with their staff members individually and collectively. If an administrator wants to keep his program moving along, he will institute those policies which are not in conflict with fundamental value systems. In fact, he may often determine practices that exist and establish policies which are in accordance with the practices.

ESTABLISHING POLICIES IN ACCORDANCE WITH PRACTICES

Example I — A Fragmentary Approach

One program administrator observed that children in several of the classes in the program were making very poor progress. The entire program was oral and the primary inhibiting factor seemed to be that the children could not function well in a totally oral environment. For one class, a particular teacher was selected, one who had proven teaching capabilities, to be sure, and who had manual communication skills. However, the teacher was not authorized, not told, to begin using manual communication. All was as it had been in terms of policy. However, after a month or so the teacher requested permission to use manual communication.

The teacher, frustrated by the failure to be able to communicate, sincerely believed the children could benefit from the incorporation of manual communication into the instructional approaches in the classroom. After a rather probing discussion, the teacher was told to prepare a rationale which, if acceptable, would be followed by a plan in order to determine the effects. She prepared a rationale, a solid case for incorporating manual communication into her instructional approach. This was followed by a plan to evaluate the results and implementation.

The results were quite positive, and not only academically. The long-term results were that other classes were gradually phased in, at teacher requests. Today, the school is, in a true sense of the term, a Total Communication school and, perhaps uniquely, includes some classes that are strictly oral. Children in the oral classes are there because they function very well. Outside the class, they communicate in the same modes as the other children. The school has built up and maintains this kind of flexibility, which is truly representative of a Total Communication philosophy. The administrator allowed (and abetted) a policy to develop which was intended to be academically nurturing for the students.

Example II — A Unitary Approach

In another school, which was totally oral, the superintendent was new. He saw a need to revise the communication modality policy and determined to do something about it. Instead of approaching his board to request a new policy, he met and agreed with the faculty that a study of communication approaches was appropriate. Toward the end of the year, the faculty report was made to the superintendent. With but one exception, the faculty was unanimous in its recommendation for a shift to Total Communication. The superintendent was requested to petition the board to establish such a policy. He never petitioned. Instead, at the next board meeting, he was presented with the results of a study the board had independently conducted and which served as the basis for a unanimous board recommendation identical to the faculty recommendation.

Both of the above examples are intended to illustrate one point. The point is that, if rationally and cooperatively attempted, a major policy change cannot only be instituted, it can become a practical working philosophy.

IMPLEMENTING THE NEW POLICY

But adopting a new policy is not the end. Rather, it is more like the beginning. A reasonable, purposeful inservice program is virtually mandatory. Simply because one recognizes the desirability of the new approach does not mean that one has the necessary skills to assist in its implementation. Teachers and others in the school, are going to need instruction, for example, in order to work toward the acquisition of, for many, new skills. What provision, further, for parent acquisition of the new communication skills will be made, if any? There could be a problem with parental acceptance, and plans must be made to work with the families.

WHICH SIGN SYSTEM SHOULD WE USE?

Usually, one of the first "big" problems arises when the question comes up of which sign system is to be used. We do not think it makes a great deal of difference and can expect some argument on that. Basically, all sign systems derive from so-called Ameslan. That is, the sign vocabulary is fundamentally the same. There are refinements, for want of a better word, which typify the systems, but here again, there is a great deal of overlap and similarity. SEE I, SEE II, LOVE, Signed English, and others purport to be systems of English in the sign modality. Also, Ameslan is not English, which might seem to be a contradiction to some people.

In the same sense that French is not English, Ameslan is not

English. That is, the syntax and grammar are not common between the two. On the other hand, some vocabulary is the same or quite similar. The syntax and grammar of Ameslan do not compare at all to English. For many years, Ameslan (by another name) was considered an inferior form of English, but modern linguists who have studied it are able to demonstrate that it is neither inferior nor superior to English; it is a different language. However, perhaps because it was so convenient to do so, we use the sign vocabulary of Ameslan and attach our English verbals (words) to signs. Ameslan is one of the few languages which does not have a spoken component nor a written component.

A determination of which system to incorporate, then, may well be of relatively small moment. What is of importance, we think, is that, whatever the system, all of the people connected with the program should be using the same system. Probably, the more complete the system, the more nearly representative of English the presentation will be. We are of the opinion that there are a number of asininities in any of the sign systems with which we are familiar. Often, it seems, it may be far more sensible to fingerspell a word than it is to sign it. Of course, this is a view from the perspective of an adult, and we really do not know whether it makes a difference for the child. Some say it does.

We often hear arguments over various facets of human behavior which may really be imponderables: processing, visual processing, is an example. What do we really know about it as it applies developmentally to the young child? In connection with this, fingerspelling is often categorized as dull, dry, lifeless, visually taxing *by adults* who never experienced fingerspelling during their developmental years. If many of us were to view manual communication in terms of meaningfulness, we might find it sadly lacking because it simply cannot be processed. By whom? By an adult just learning sign. So what does that prove? Nothing. Nothing, because there is likely very little relationship between the matured organism (the adult) and the immature organism (the child) in developmental terms.

Somehow, we have to obtain objective data which will

permit us to understand basic questions in terms of the development of children. Have we ever addressed the problem of different approaches for visually oriented versus auditorily oriented learners? How many serious attempts have been made to find ways to identify one from the other? What about an auditorily oriented learner who is deaf or a visually oriented learner who is blind? We seem to be straying again, but we do want to try to make the point that there are problems to be confronted we have not even as yet identified, and oftentimes we assume that behavior which may be true for the adult is similarly true for the child; a potentially dangerously misleading assumption.

INCORPORATING A SIGN SYSTEM INTO OUR COMMUNICATIVE BEHAVIOR

Assuming that we have enabled our teachers and others to develop manual communication skills and that we have agreed upon a particular sign system, incorporation of the manual modes into our communication behavior with the children remains. Once again, there are potential pitfalls, as we see it, which could result in seriously retarding the deaf child's progress toward mastery of the English language.

One of these potential pitfalls may be represented by the often-asked question, "How do we teach the children the signs?" Apparently a very good question. But, in terms of human behavior and development, is it valid? The question implies that it is necessary to teach, in the formal sense, the signs to the children. Frankly, it would appear to us that if we instituted a program of formally teaching sign vocabulary to deaf children, in much the same way we teach reading or speech vocabulary, we can pretty well expect minimal results. Contrast this notion with the way normally hearing children acquire their vocabularies. If we were to concentrate our efforts on teaching normally hearing children their vocabularies from the moment of birth, think of what we could probably accomplish. We would want to select only that vocabulary which would be "meaningful" for the child and stay with it until he could reproduce it himself. By the time he was twelve to fifteen months old, very likely he would be well ahead of children who were not being formally taught. By the time he reached the age of four or five, he would probably be significantly behind and, more importantly, might be limited in his linguistic structure to noun-verb sentences and a few noun-verb where or when clause sentences.

We are all aware that, in the formal sense, teaching of language to normally hearing children during their developmental years would in all probability be foolhardy. They *acquire* an understanding of language and ability to use the language primarily because of the meaningful experiences they have had almost from birth. We are aware that they have even mastered the rules for the language and are applying those rules with near syntactic perfection by the time they are four or five years old. But nobody ever *taught* them. They learned because they were in an environment of language which was meaningful and fully available to them.

If we want the deaf child, and the younger he is the more relevant the point, to master English, we must do everything we possibly can to assure him a language environment which is meaningful to him and as fully available as it is possible to make it. We do not have to plan which vocabulary we will instruct him in. We do not have to help him identify vocabulary with the parts of the Fitzgerald Key. We do have to talk to him and around him. Thus, since we are discussing Total Communication, the school, and home, whenever possible, should have people in them who use Total Communication totally. Now that is not easy.

If you wish to teach the deaf child, the young deaf child especially, provide him with the models of language with which he can parallel the developmental stages the normally hearing child goes through. So, in answer to the question, "How do you teach the children the signs?," we believe, "You don't. You give him the opportunity to learn." This is easy to say. In addition, we must always bear in mind the fact that we do not demand vocabulary, etc., from the underdeveloped normally hearing child and we must, similarly, not make inappropriate demands on the deaf child. Demands should always be consistent with the child's level of development.

A STRUCTURED APPROACH MIGHT BE NEEDED

Nonetheless, suppose you are confronted with deaf children who are almost totally undeveloped as far as true language acquisition is concerned? Perhaps children who are twelve, thirteen, or fourteen years of age or older are encountered. Perhaps they have never been to school or have been in environments which were totally incomprehensible to them as far as language is concerned. Obviously, it would seem, a more structured approach would be necessary. A language therapy program, a formal, structured approach to language development would almost certainly *have* to be available. But, still, it should be in addition to a meaningful language environment. In other words, we still must provide the Total Communication environment, as well as a carefully organized, sequential language therapy program. Realistically, the older the child before he is in such an environment, the less likely it is that he will ever achieve the norm in language skill.

MANUAL COMMUNICATION AS A SUBJECT OF STUDY

There is still another aspect to be considered, which is that there very likely could or should be provision in the school program for manual communication as a subject area. Simply because a child is deaf does not guarantee mastery of sign. Formal instruction may well be indicated. In addition to this, such a provision could afford the students opportunity to experience the aesthetics, such as in drama and poetry-music, especially. The children would be able to develop an added dimension in their lives which could open up other worlds for them and help enrich their lives culturally. And, there would be an opportunity to develop an appreciation for manual communication as it might relate to personal feelings of esteem.

An Example of Manual Communication

Not too long ago, there was a workshop in manual communication which had an evaluation component built in. One of the items in the evaluation was concerned with the question of Ameslan as a language. Most of the deaf people in that workshop indicated that they did not think Ameslan was a language. It is not important that the thinking was in error. What is important for the adult deaf people, most of whom had earned college undergraduate and graduate degrees, is the reason behind the answer that Ameslan is not a language. We will not pretend to know the reason, but we cannot help but wonder whether such an attitude might not result from the old thinking that, "signing is bad." How would we feel if, from early in our lives and for twelve to fifteen years thereafter, we were constantly told not to talk; to write because talking is bad or nasty or dirty? If we are hammered away at by authoritative people, consistently on one point, we are bound to be affected.

Perhaps many deaf people do feel inferior because they do not speak well enough and feel very defensive because they have to rely on manual communication to understand. If so, it may well be that the "superiors" in their earlier years, school authorities, stressed oral skills so much and denigrated signing. Children were punished for signing in those "dark ages." In our view, it is analogous to denying the blind child braille reading when we deny the deaf child the language of signs.

THE NEED FOR A HEALTHY SELF-CONCEPT

Self-concept is extremely important. It should be obvious that we should seek ways to assist the children we work with in developing a healthy self-concept. Under a Total Communication approach, the modalities which enable us to do so exist.

SPECIFIC CONSIDERATIONS IN IMPLEMENTING A TOTAL COMMUNICATIONS PROGRAM

Let us now assume that we are at the stage where we can agree that Total Communication is appropriate and desirable in our programs for deaf children. We will assume that all the school personnel and all the family members agree and wish to

develop the necessary added communication skills. We, therefore, have planned appropriate inservice and parent education
programs. The program has to succeed.

Does the program mean that we sign and fingerspell everything we say in the classroom? Does it mean that this is all we
really have to do? Are there times and places when we do not
sign and fingerspell? If so, what are they? How rapidly should I
sign and spell? Or, how slowly? Do I want to be consistent in
my delivery rate? Or, should I vary the rate? If so, in what ways
and for what reasons? How do I know I have the necessary
attributes to be a successful signer or speller? What do I do if I
cannot keep up with the children? Let us try to deal with some
of these questions.

Do We Sign and Spell Everything in the Classroom?

To this, we can only say that only the teacher can or should
decide to sign or spell everything in the classroom. But, at the
same time, it is a decision which must be made on a profes-
sional basis. For the most part, of course, it would be virtually
mandatory that we use all forms in nearly all group instruction. But, maybe there are one or two children who seem to
have a good capability for speechreading. The teacher might
want to seize upon opportunities when working with only this
child to discontinue the manual forms in order to help rein-
force his progress in speechreading development. Certainly, use
manual forms as needed, but why not give him controlled
experience in relying on speechreading alone?

Is the Only Difference in Our Programs That We Now Use Manual Communication?

Is this the only thing that changes? Again, the teacher can
best answer that. But, consider, if Total Communication really
does make a difference in the level of language skills, will there
be a concomitant effect on the rate of progress academically? It
may well mean a wholesale revision of the entire curriculum.
When we asked for Total Communication, we may have
thought we were asking for an inch. Suddenly, like it or not,

we may have gotten the whole mile. Our old concepts of what constitutes the curricular needs for deaf children, almost from the outset, are in for a real shaking up — that is, assuming that Total Communication approaches are, indeed, effective.

In a true Total Communication environment, are there times or places where manual modes may be discontinued? We are thinking now of circumstances in which the children are not actively concerned.

An Example — Discontinuation of Manual Modes

Suppose the principal comes into the teacher's classroom with a message. If it were a classroom for normally hearing children, most of the children would be able to overhear what the teacher and principal were saying. Generally, we have observed that the usual procedure in classes for deaf children is a totally oral exchange. It is our view that we are attempting to provide a completely parallel environment under Total Communication procedures and it is, therefore, mandatory that what is spoken orally in this situation, and others, should be said using manual modes as well. In fact, as long as we are in the environment, whether children are involved directly notwithstanding, we should be using all modes all the time. Certainly there are exceptions, such as when in conference behind closed doors, but as a general rule, Total Communication should mean that we are providing as total a language environment as possible. So, our suggestion is to use the manual modes in all parallel circumstances in which normally hearing children would have access to what is being said. As the posters put out by the Education Today Company* remind us, "No one ever said teaching was going to be easy."

What About Speed — Is There A Desirable Speed At Which We Should Be Attempting To Use Manual Modes?

There may be a desirable speed for manual modes, but it is

---

*Education Today Co. Inc., 530 Univ. Ave., Palo Alto, California 94301 doubtful we know what it is. Some of us may be limited to a relatively slow speed simply because of our lack of facility manually. On the other hand, some people develop such facility that it may well be they tend to go too rapidly. We could be less concerned about the slower signers because it is highly unlikely the children will be slighted. The more facile signers, on the other hand, probably need to take extra care that the speed is not more than the children can handle. We do not mean that the children should perceive every single word any more than we would expect a normally hearing child to get all words. We do mean that we want to ensure the children have the opportunity to understand as fully as possible under reasonable conditions.

At the same time, some people feel that using manual communication slows things down so much that we really cannot cover the ground. That is, if only speech is used, we can go much faster. This may be true, but if the child is unable to understand, what has been saved? If anything, rather than conserving time, we are in serious danger of wasting a great deal more. Our preference, always, is to speak only as rapidly as we can comfortably sign, but if we feel even that is too fast, we should slow down our manual communication components, also. To paraphrase a popular cliché, "Different strokes for different circumstances."

ACQUIRING THE NECESSARY SKILLS

The final question we have suggested has to do with whether the neophyte in Total Communication has the necessary attributes to be successful with the manual modes. For many people, this is a point for great concern. Usually, the beginner wonders about his ability to learn and use manual modes. He feels awkward, cannot seem to remember the sign, is an inaccurate speller under the best of conditions, and feels very self-conscious, etc. Fundamentally, we have not met anyone who, having put forth the effort, cannot learn to use manual modes sufficiently well. But, this is an area which needs attention in any inservice program, and the fact is, there *could* be some people who will not be able to acquire the skills.

Usually, after having gotten into manual communication and reaching the point where one can use it, the next (and bigger) crisis is likely to occur. Suddenly, or not so suddenly, one begins to realize the enormity of the task of learning to read. In terms of receptive skill, some of us may be illiterate, or functionally so, when it comes to the give-and-take of manual communication. How many of us can read fingerspelling? How many deaf persons do you know who can read it comfortably, with ease? How many of us can fingerspell? How many can sign? How many can keep up in conversation with a deaf person? Why do we have so much difficulty understanding?

Basically, it seems that the poor reader is "hung up" on trying to read manual communication. That is, he tries to capture every sign, every fingerspelled letter and hold all the information until he can put it together meaningfully. In our experience, this is a technique for learning to read which almost certainly guarantees failure. Our success in teaching people to read comes when they follow instructions to just view and to make no attempt to gather it all in. At the beginning, and for varying lengths of time, potential illiterates make little to no progress receptively. But they continue to follow instructions and one day, almost like having the ability conferred upon them, the vast majority, faces beaming, tell us the good news, "I can read." This pleases us and makes us sad, because we are still trying to achieve a decent level of literacy.

A FINAL THOUGHT

As was implied earlier, there are still many questions. Also, there is much research still to be done in an attempt to answer questions. Not only that, there are many questions, we feel sure, we have not even uncovered yet. It is our hope that this discussion has been helpful in providing you with a clearer perspective. In the areas which were dealt with, we have attempted to argue for meaningful communication opportunity for every child, based on the individual child's needs and capabilities. It may be difficult to accomplish, but we think each child is worth our best efforts.

REFERENCES

1. Richard W. Hostrop, *Managing Education for Results,* 2nd ed. (Homewood, Illinois: ETC Publications, 1975), pp. 3-4.
2. David E. Barbee and Aubrey J. Bouck, *Accountability in Education* (New York: Petrocelli Books, 1974), p. xiv.
3. Hostrop, p. 237.
4. *Ibid.,* pp. 21-47.
5. H. D. Babbidge, Jr., *Education of the Deaf* (Washington, D.C.: U.S. Department of Health, Education, and Welfare, 1965).
6. Jerome D. Schein and Marcus T. Delk, Jr., *The Deaf Population of the United States* (Silver Spring, Maryland: National Association of the Deaf, 1974).
7. I. K. Jordan, Gerilee Gustason, Roslyn Rosen, "Current Communication Trends at Programs for the Deaf," *American Annals of the Deaf, 121*:527-532, 1976.
8. Babbidge.
9. K. P. Meadow, "Early Manual Communication in Relation to the Deaf Child's Intellectual, Social, and Communicative Function." *American Annals of the Deaf, 113*:29-41, 1968.
10. McCay Vernon and S. Koh, "Early Manual Communication and the Deaf Child's Achievement," *American Annals of the Deaf, 115*:527-536, 1970.
11. M. Kent, "Total Communication at the Maryland School for the Deaf," *Deaf American, 23*:5-8, 1971.
12. Hilde S. Schlesinger and Kathryn P. Meadow, *Sound and Sign: Childhood Deafness and Mental Health* (Berkeley: University of California Press, 1972).
13. D. Moores et al., *Evaluation of Programs for Hearing Impaired Children* (University of Minnesota Research, Development, and Demonstration Center in Education of the Handicapped Children, Series 1971-1975.)
14. M. A. Herx and F. E. Hunt, "A Framework for Speech Development Within a Total Communication System," *American Annals of the Deaf, 121*:553-540, 1976.
15. Jordan, Gustason, and Rosen.

— CHAPTER 6 —

CONCLUSION — WHY TOTAL
COMMUNICATION?

THERE are some people who claim that
Total Communication is nothing new, merely a misnomer, a
case of "word juggling" for the older method of the combined
system.[1] Total Communication is criticized as a "simple solu-
tion" to a "complex problem . . . [with a] sort of superficial
surface appeal,"[2] or a "curious mixture which cannot blend,"[3]
or simply "a fraud."[4] Such criticisms result from an erroneous
perception of the philosophy. Total Communication is not
synonymous with the combined method of instruction. As we
have tried to illustrate, Total Communication is a philosophy
which supports any system of instruction which best benefits
the deaf child.

There is really no other philosphy which has recommended
the utilization of all modes of communication input advocated
in Total Communication. This is what the new philosophy is
all about — input. In simple terms, Total Communication
recognizes "the right of a deaf child to learn to use *all* forms of
communication available to develop language competence.
This includes the full spectrum, child devised gestures, speech,
formal signs, fingerspelling, speechreading, reading and
writing. To every deaf child should also be provided the opportunity to learn to use any remnant of residual hearing he may
have by employing the best possible electronic equipment for
amplifying sound."[5]

Implicit in the Total Communication philosophy is the idea
that all avenues of communication will be employed.[6] Under-
lying the philosophy are the following assumptions:

  1. Language development is a product of communication,
     and communication grows out of interaction. Language is
     a product of dialogue rather than instruction.[7]

2. There is a natural sequence in the levels of linguistic development common to all people. This linguistic process cannot be postponed nor its natural sequence arbitrarily interrupted or altered without serious consequences.[8]
3. The time for optimum linguistic growth and development is during infancy and early childhood. Thus, the home and family assume an initial responsibility for the child's linguistic development.[9]
4. Ideas and concepts precede words in the linguistic experience of the individual. These basic concepts can more readily be integrated into the child's language experience when the symbols used tend to illustrate or describe the concepts they represent. For the deaf child, these concept-based symbols are signs. Signs become the initial tools for linguistic interaction between parent and child.[10]
5. The act of communication is more important than how one communicates.[11]

As Dr. Lloyd indicated in Chapter 5, "The first priority in the education of deaf children is education." With such a priority in mind we should do whatever is necessary to achieve this objective — *education.* Through the philosophy of Total Communication and the resources it makes available to us, we have a better chance of reaching that goal. Total Communication is nothing more than an attempt to expand education opportunities for deaf children.

We must concur with Boyce R. Williams, Director, Office of Deafness and Communicative Disorders, Rehabilitation Services Administration. While speaking on behalf of the deaf community about the new philosophy, Williams stated, "Total Communication represents the great emancipation of deaf people from an inadequate, sterile, educational system."[12]

REFERENCES

1. Helen S. Lane, "Thoughts on Oral Advocacy Today . . . With Memories of the Society of Oral Advocates," *Volta Review, 78,* 3:137, 1976.
2. Daniel Ling, "Statements of Mr. Ling on Panel of Reactors on

Oralism/Auralism and 'Total Communication'," *Volta Review, 74,* 9:554, 1973.

3. J. K. Reeves, "Scope or Oralism," *Volta Review, 29, 1*:50, 1977.

4. Philip R. Drum, "Total Communication — Fraud or Reality?" *Volta Review, 74, 9*:564, 1972.

5. David M. Denton, "Remarks in Support of a System of Total Communication for Deaf Children." In *Communication Symposium* (Frederick, Maryland: Maryland School for the Deaf, 1970), p. 5.

6. *Ibid.,* pp. 5-6.

7. David M. Denton, "Total Communication ... Definition," *Deaf Spectrum, 4, 3*:10-11, 1973.

8. *Ibid.,* p. 11.

9. *Ibid.*

10. *Ibid.*

11. "Excerpts From Talks of: Roy K. Holcomb ...," *Deaf Spectrum, 4, 5*:5, 1973.

12. Boyce R. Williams, "Some Thoughts on Total Communication." In *Communication Symposium* (Frederick, Maryland: Maryland School for the Deaf, 1970), p. 15.

APPENDICES

CURRENT COMMUNICATION TRENDS AT PROGRAMS FOR THE DEAF*†

$\mathbf{D}$URING the 1975-1976 school year, a national survey of schools and classes for the hearing impaired was conducted to ascertain the various communication modes used in the classroom. The following tables represent the results of this survey.

TABLE A-I.

TOTAL NUMBER OF PROGRAMS REPORTING PRIMARY USE
OF THE FOUR MODES OF COMMUNICATION AT
DIFFERENT SCHOOL LEVELS

	Preschool	Elementary	Junior High School	High School
Total Number of Progrems With Classes at Each Level	552	625	369	305
Cued Speech	9	8	6	7
Oral-Aural	284	341	195	148
Rochester Method	10	13	9	6
Total Communication	324	411	212	192
Total	627	773	422	353

*From I. K. Jordan, Gerilee Gustason, and Roslyn Rosen, "Current Communication Trends at Programs for the Deaf," *American Annals of the Deaf, 121, 6*:1976. Courtesy of *American Annals of the Deaf*, Washington, D.C.

†The authors of this survey report emphasize that the rapidity of change, as indicated in the report, means that such information is quickly outdated. However, the fact that there are such rapid changes in the area of communication modes utilized for deaf children is apparent from the study.

TABLE A-II.

TOTAL NUMBER OF CLASSES REPORTING PRIMARY USE
OF THE FOUR MODES OF COMMUNICATION AT
DIFFERENT SCHOOL LEVELS

	Preschool	Elementary	Junior High School	High School
Cued Speech	10	14	6	7
Oral-Aural	522	1,240	359	249
Rochester Method	38	72	33	12
Total Communication	689	2,196	688	1,046
Total	1,259	3,522	1,086	1,314

TABLE A-III.

THE NUMBER OF PROGRAMS REPORTING CHANGES
FROM (PREVIOUS) AND TO (PRESENT) THE
DIFFERENT COMMUNICATION MODES

	Preschool (Prev.)(Pres.)		Elementary (Prev.) (Pres.)		Junior High School (Prev.)(Pres.)		High School (Prev.)(Pres.)	
Cued Speech	2	0	3	0	1	0	1	0
Oral-Aural	90	3	131	1	44	1	37	0
Rochester	1	1	1	0	1	0	0	0
Total Communication	5	97	2	138	1	52	0	46
Other	4	3	2	1	4	0	6	0

SCHOOL ACHIEVEMENT SCORES OF HEARING-IMPAIRED CHILDREN; NATIONAL DATA ON ACHIEVEMENT STATUS AND GROWTH PATTERNS*

FIGURES B-1 and B-2 provide visual summaries of the national distributions of achievement scores of hearing-impaired children in the subjects of reading comprehension and math computation, respectively.

The lines in each figure represent the 10th, 25th, 75th, and 90th percentile points of the distribution for hearing-impaired children. For purposes of comparison, the mean score for each age for the national standardization sample of hearing children is shown as a sixth line. The norm line for hearing children is a mean rather than a median (50th percentile) and appears only for those ages for which national data are available. In Figure B-1, the norm line for hearing children is based on actual data for all ages shown, whereas in Figure B-2, actual data were available only for ages 8.6 and 13.6 years. The remainder of the norm line is based on extrapolation.

The achievement scores on the vertical axes are in terms of scaled scores rather than the more familiar grade equivalents. The scaled score is a more accurate measure and is the most appropriate method available for combining scores across test levels to produce score distributions for particular age-groups. The scaled scores are based on two anchor points. A scaled score of 132 was set equal to a grade equivalent score of 3.2, and a scaled score of 182 was set equal to a grade equivalent of 8.2. The five years' time between these two points was then divided by the fifty scaled score points, so that each scaled score point represents one fiftieth of five years' growth, or the *average*

---

*From Raymond J. Trybus and Michael A. Karchmer, A report. Courtesy of the Office of Demographic Studies, Gallaudet College, Washington, D.C.

growth per academic month over this time period. Because academic growth does not proceed at an even pace (more growth occurs in some months than in others), one scaled score point is not necessarily equal to one month in grade equivalence. In general, the closer a scaled score is to either anchor point, the more exactly it corresponds to the similarly numbered grade equivalent; as the scaled score moves above, below, or between these two anchor points, it corresponds less exactly to the similarly numbered grade equivalent.

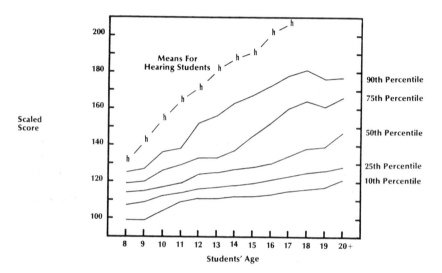

Figure B-1. Reading comprehension scores national distribution for hearing-impaired students. Half of the twenty-year-old deaf student population reads under the mid-fourth-grade level. Only 10 percent of hearing-impaired eighteen-year-olds can read above an eighth-grade level. From Raymond J. Trybus and Michael A. Karchmer, School Achievement Scores of Hearing Impaired Children: National Data on Achievement Status and Growth Patterns, *American Annals of the Deaf, 122,* 2:62-69, 1977.

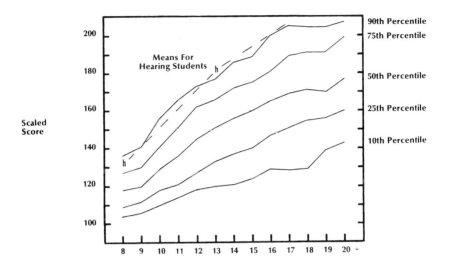

Figure B-2. Mathematics computation scores national distribution for hearing-impaired students. With respect to mathematics computations, 10 percent of hearing-impaired children reach the level of difficulty attained by the average hearing child of the same age, but the majority are still way below their hearing counterparts. From Raymond J. Trybus and Michael A. Karchmer, School Achievement Scores of Hearing Impaired Children: National Data on Achievement Status and Growth Patterns, *American Annals of the Deaf, 122,* 2:62-69, 1977.

INDEX

111